White Fang

*A Wild and Heartfelt Story of Trust,
Transformation & the Bond Between Beast and
Man*

A Modern Translation
Adapted for the Contemporary Reader

Jack London

Translated by Tim Zengerink

Table of Contents

Preface
Message to the Reader

Rebuilding the Greatest Library in Human History

Thousands of years ago, the Library of Alexandria was the heart of global knowledge — a sanctuary where the wisdom of every known civilization was gathered and shared freely.

And then, it was lost.

Now, we're rebuilding it — and you are invited to join us.

At the Library of Alexandria, we've set out to make every book available to every person on Earth — not just in print, but in every language, every format, and for every reader.

Here's how we do it:

- **Deluxe Print Editions at True Printing Cost** - Order any book as a high-quality paperback, elegant hardcover, or stunning boxset — and only pay what it costs to print. No markups. No middlemen.
- **Unlimited Access to the Greatest Works** - Enjoy thousands of timeless classics — from Plato to Shakespeare to Tolstoy — in beautiful, modern eBook and audiobook editions. Read and listen without limits — for every reader, everywhere.
- **Modern Translations for Every Language & Dialect** - We're reimagining the classics in clear, accessible language — and translating them into every dialect imaginable. Everyone deserves to understand humanity's greatest ideas.

When you visit **LibraryofAlexandria.com**, you're not just accessing books — you're joining a global movement to restore, preserve, and share the wisdom of civilization.

Join us today at LibraryofAlexandria.com

Together, we'll ensure the light of human wisdom never fades again.

With gratitude,

The Modern Library of Alexandria Team

Visit:
www.libraryofalexandria.com
Or scan the code below:

Introduction

From Wilderness to Civilization:
The Core of White Fang

Few novels have captured the raw, untamed spirit of the wilderness while simultaneously exploring the depths of trust, loyalty, and transformation as profoundly as Jack London's White Fang. First published in 1906, this companion piece to London's earlier masterpiece, *The Call of the Wild*, reverses the narrative arc of its predecessor. While *The Call of the Wild* tells the story of a domesticated dog returning to the wild, White Fang chronicles the journey of a wild wolf-dog as he is drawn—often painfully—into the world of humans, learning to navigate not only survival but also affection, morality, and ultimately, love.

Set during the Klondike Gold Rush of the 1890s, *White Fang* is a gripping narrative that explores the stark realities of life in the Yukon Territory, where the environment is unforgiving and survival often depends on brute strength, cunning, and adaptability. But beneath its adventure-filled surface, the novel is a profound reflection on the relationship between nature and nurture, violence and compassion, freedom and domestication. It is a story about how living beings—whether animal or human—can be shaped by both the harshness of their environment and the redemptive power of kindness.

Jack London's own life experiences deeply inform *White Fang*. Born into poverty in 1876, London was a self-taught adventurer, laborer, sailor, and gold prospector before achieving literary fame. His time in the Yukon during the gold rush gave him firsthand knowledge of the brutal conditions of the North, and this authenticity permeates his writing. The icy landscapes, the danger-laden trails, and the struggle for food and survival are depicted with a realism that could only come from lived experience. Yet London was not content to simply write adventure stories. In *White Fang*, he sought to explore larger philosophical questions—about evolution, the nature of violence, and the capacity for both animals and humans to change.

The story of *White Fang* begins in the harsh, frozen wilderness where a she-wolf and her mate struggle to survive, giving birth to a litter in which only one pup survives—the titular White Fang. From the moment of his birth, White Fang's life is defined by the struggle between his wild instincts and the forces of his environment. London masterfully portrays the wolf-dog's early encounters with hunger, danger, and other animals, painting a vivid picture of the "law of the wild," where only the strongest, smartest, and most adaptable creatures thrive.

As White Fang grows, his life takes a dramatic turn when he is captured by humans. This marks the beginning of the novel's exploration of the tension between feral independence and domestication. White Fang's early experiences with humans are brutal. He is beaten, exploited, and forced into dogfighting—a cruel "entertainment" that was prevalent during the gold rush era. These experiences harden him, making him distrustful of humans and reinforcing his reliance on aggression as a means of survival.

But London does not leave his protagonist trapped in this cycle of violence. Through the character of Weedon Scott—a compassionate and patient man who rescues White Fang from his abusive owner—London introduces the transformative power of love and trust. Under Scott's care, White Fang slowly learns to accept kindness, to trust humans, and to form bonds that go beyond instinctual loyalty. This transformation is at the heart of the novel, serving as both a narrative climax and a philosophical statement about the capacity for redemption and change.

Themes of Survival, Trust, and Transformation

At its core, *White Fang* is a novel about survival—not only in the physical sense but also in the emotional and psychological sense. London vividly portrays the harsh realities of life in the wild, where every day is a struggle for food, shelter, and safety. The "law of the fang" governs the animal world, where strength, cunning, and ferocity determine who lives and who dies. White Fang learns this law early, and it shapes his understanding of the world. He grows up knowing that kindness is a rarity and that violence is often the only means of survival.

However, as the story progresses, London contrasts this brutal law of the wild with what might be called the "law of love." Through Weedon Scott's patience and compassion, White Fang learns that life can be governed by cooperation, trust, and mutual care. This transformation is not easy; it is marked by setbacks, moments of fear, and the deep-seated instinct to revert to aggression. Yet London's portrayal of this process is both moving and profound. It suggests that even the most hardened creatures—whether animal or human—are capable of change when they are met with understanding and kindness.

Another central theme of *White Fang* is the tension between nature and nurture. London, heavily influenced by Charles Darwin's theory of evolution and Herbert Spencer's concept of "survival of the fittest," believed that environment plays a crucial role in shaping behavior and character. In the early chapters, White Fang is a product of the wild, guided by instincts honed by generations of survival in harsh conditions. But as he comes into contact with humans, he begins to change—not because his instincts disappear, but because his environment teaches him new ways of living.

This theme resonates beyond the animal world. London is also commenting on human society, where individuals are often shaped by the conditions in which they are raised. The novel implicitly asks whether violence, cruelty, and mistrust are innate or whether they are the products of harsh environments. By showing White Fang's transformation under the influence of compassion, London suggests that nurture can play a transformative role, offering a hopeful counterpoint to the often bleak realities of survival.

The novel also explores the relationship between humans and animals, a relationship that is both symbiotic and fraught with tension. Humans in *White Fang* are not depicted as inherently good or evil; they range from cruel exploiters like Beauty Smith, who forces White Fang into dogfighting, to kind-hearted individuals like Weedon Scott. London's portrayal of these characters underscores the idea that the treatment of animals reflects broader values within human society. Compassionate treatment leads to loyalty and harmony, while cruelty breeds fear and aggression.

Finally, *White Fang* can be read as a meditation on transformation and identity. The titular character is not static; he evolves throughout the novel, moving from a wild, feral creature to a loyal companion and protector. This transformation is not simply about domestication; it is about learning to trust, to connect, and to find meaning in relationships. In this sense, White Fang is as much about the emotional journey of its protagonist as it is about his physical survival.

London's Style, Legacy, and the Reader's Experience

Jack London's writing style in *White Fang* is characterized by vivid, almost cinematic descriptions of the natural world. His prose is both poetic and precise, capturing the beauty and brutality of the Yukon landscape in equal measure. London's ability to convey the thoughts and instincts of animals without anthropomorphizing them excessively is one of the novel's greatest strengths. He gives readers a sense of White Fang's inner world—his fears, desires, and instincts—while still maintaining the realism of an animal's perspective.

The structure of the novel is carefully crafted to reflect White Fang's journey. The early chapters, set entirely in the wild, are almost devoid of human presence, focusing instead on the rhythms of nature and the struggle for survival. As the story progresses and humans enter the narrative, the focus shifts to the interaction between man and beast, culminating in the transformative relationship between White Fang and Weedon Scott. This gradual shift mirrors White Fang's own journey from wilderness to civilization.

London's legacy as a writer is deeply tied to works like White Fang. His ability to blend adventure with philosophical depth, realism with emotional resonance, has ensured that his novels remain widely read and studied. *White Fang*, in particular, has endured because it appeals to readers on multiple levels. It is an exciting adventure story, filled with danger and suspense, but it is also a moving exploration of trust, redemption, and the bond between humans and animals.

For modern readers, *White Fang* offers not just a window into the rugged life of the Yukon during the gold rush, but also timeless lessons about resilience, compassion, and the transformative power of kindness. It challenges us to consider how we treat animals and, by extension, how we treat one another. It reminds us that trust is not given lightly but earned through patience and care, and that even the most hardened beings can change when shown genuine understanding.

As you begin reading *White Fang*, immerse yourself in the vivid landscapes that London so brilliantly depicts—the icy rivers, the dense forests, the unforgiving winters. Pay attention to White Fang's gradual transformation, noting how each encounter, whether with a wolf, a dog, or a human, shapes his character. Observe the contrasts between the harshness of his early life and the warmth of his eventual bond with Weedon Scott. And, above all, allow yourself to feel the emotional weight of this journey—a journey that is both a thrilling adventure and a heartfelt meditation on trust and transformation.

Part I

Chapter I: The Trail of The Meat

Dark spruce trees loomed menacingly on both sides of the frozen waterway. Recent winds had stripped away their white frost coating, leaving them appearing to lean toward one another, black and threatening in the dimming light. Complete silence blanketed the landscape. The land stretched out as a barren wasteland, devoid of life and motion, so isolated and frigid that its essence transcended even sorrow. Something within it suggested laughter, yet this was a laughter far more frightening than any grief—a joyless laughter like the enigmatic smile of the sphinx, as cold as ice and carrying the harsh certainty of fate. This was the commanding and indescribable wisdom of eternity mocking life's pointlessness and all human struggle. This was the wilderness, the untamed, cold-hearted northern frontier.

But there was life, moving through the land and refusing to surrender. Down the frozen waterway struggled a team of wolf-like dogs. Their coarse fur was covered with frost. Their breath turned to ice in the air as it escaped their mouths, shooting out in clouds of vapor that landed on their body hair and turned into frost crystals. The dogs wore leather harnesses, and leather straps connected them to a sled that they pulled behind them. The sled had no runners. It was built from thick birch bark, and its entire bottom surface lay flat on the snow. The front of the sled curved upward, like a rolled piece of paper, to push down and underneath the pile of soft snow that rolled like a wave in front of it. On the sled, tied down tightly, sat a long and narrow rectangular box. Other items were loaded on the sled—blankets, an axe, a coffee pot and a frying pan—but standing out and taking up most of the room was the long and narrow rectangular box.

Ahead of the dogs, wearing broad snowshoes, a man struggled forward through the snow. Behind the sled, a second man labored along. On the sled, inside the box, lay a third man whose struggle had ended—a man the wilderness had defeated and crushed until he would never move or fight again. The wilderness doesn't welcome movement. Life offends it because life means movement, and the wilderness always seeks to stop all motion. It freezes water to keep it from flowing to the ocean; it forces the sap from trees until they freeze to their core; and most savagely and ruthlessly of all, the wilderness hunts down and forces into surrender man— man who represents life's greatest restlessness, forever rebelling against the law that all movement must eventually stop.

But at the front and back, fearless and unbreakable, worked the two men who were still alive. Their bodies were wrapped in fur and soft leather. Their eyelashes, cheeks, and lips were so covered with ice crystals from their frozen breath that you couldn't make out their faces. This made them look like ghostly masks, like funeral directors in a supernatural world burying some spirit. But underneath it all, they were human beings, pushing through a land of emptiness, scorn, and silence—small explorers attempting an enormous journey, fighting against the power of a world as distant and strange and lifeless as the depths of outer space.

They continued their journey in silence, conserving their energy for the physical demands ahead. All around them stretched an overwhelming quiet that seemed to have substance and weight. This silence affected their thoughts the same way crushing water pressure impacts a deep-sea diver's body. It overwhelmed them with the burden of endless space and unchangeable natural laws. The silence forced them deep into the hidden corners of their minds, squeezing out all their artificial passions, false excitement, and inflated sense of self-importance like juice pressed from grapes, until they saw themselves as they truly were: limited and tiny, mere particles of dust moving with feeble cleverness and little understanding among the vast, indifferent forces of nature.

An hour passed, and then another hour. The dim light of the brief, sunless day was starting to fade when a faint, distant cry rose through the still air. It climbed upward with a rapid surge until it reached its highest pitch, where it lingered, trembling and taut, before slowly fading away. It could have been the wail of a lost soul, except it carried a certain melancholy fierceness and ravenous longing. The man in front turned his head until his gaze met the eyes of the man behind him. Then, across the narrow rectangular box, each gave the other a nod.

A second cry rang out, cutting through the silence with a sharp, piercing shrillness. Both men pinpointed where the sound was coming from. It came from behind them, somewhere in the snowy wasteland they had just crossed. A third cry responded, also coming from behind them but to the left of where the second cry had originated.

"They're coming for us, Bill," said the man in front.

His voice sounded rough and strange, and it seemed like speaking required considerable effort from him.

"Meat is hard to find," his companion replied. "I haven't seen any rabbit tracks for days."

Thereafter they spoke no more, though their ears remained alert for the hunting cries that continued to echo behind them.

When darkness fell, they guided the dogs into a grove of spruce trees beside the waterway and set up camp. The coffin, positioned next to the fire, functioned as both a seat and a table. The wolf-dogs gathered on the opposite side of the fire, growling and quarreling with one another, but showed no desire to wander off into the darkness.

"It seems to me, Henry, they're staying remarkably close to camp," Bill commented.

Henry crouched over the fire, steadying the coffee pot with a chunk of ice, and gave a nod. He remained silent until he had settled himself on the coffin and started eating.

"They know where they can stay safe," he said. "They'd rather eat food than become food themselves. Those dogs are pretty smart."

Bill shook his head. "Oh, I don't know."

His companion looked at him with curiosity. "This is the first time I've ever heard you say anything about them not being wise."

"Henry," said the other man, chewing his beans slowly and deliberately, "did you happen to notice how those dogs got all worked up when I was feeding them?"

"They were more disruptive than usual," Henry acknowledged.

"How many dogs do we have, Henry?"

"Six."

"Well, Henry..." Bill paused for a moment, wanting his words to carry more weight. "Like I was saying, Henry, we have six dogs. I took six fish out of the bag. I gave one fish to each dog, and Henry, I came up one fish short."

"You counted wrong."

"We have six dogs," the other repeated without emotion. "I took out six fish. One Ear didn't get any fish. I came back to the bag afterward and got him his fish."

"We only have six dogs," Henry said.

"Henry," Bill continued. "I'm not saying they were all worthless, but seven of them managed to catch fish."

Henry paused his meal to look across the fire and count the dogs.

"There are only six now," he said.

"I saw the other one run off across the snow," Bill announced with cool positiveness. "I saw seven."

Henry looked at him with sympathy and said, "I'll be incredibly relieved when this trip is finished."

"What do you mean by that?" Bill demanded.

"I mean that this burden we're carrying is getting on your nerves, and you're starting to see things."

"I thought of that," Bill replied seriously. "And so, when I saw it run off across the snow, I looked in the snow and saw its tracks. Then I counted the dogs and there were still six of them. The tracks are there in the snow now. Do you want to look at them? I'll show them to you."

Henry didn't respond, but continued eating quietly until he finished his meal, ending it with one last cup of coffee. He wiped his mouth with the back of his hand and said:

"Then you're thinking that it was—"

A long, wailing cry—fierce and heartbreaking—echoed from somewhere in the darkness, cutting him off mid-sentence. He paused to listen, then completed his thought with a gesture toward where the sound had come from, "—one of them?"

Bill nodded. "I'd much rather believe that than anything else. You noticed the commotion the dogs made yourself."

Shout after shout, with responding calls, transformed the quiet into complete chaos. The cries came from all directions, and the dogs showed their terror by pressing together so tightly near the fire that the flames singed their fur. Bill added more wood to the fire before he lit his pipe.

"I'm thinking you're feeling pretty down," Henry said.

"Henry . . . " He drew thoughtfully on his pipe for a while before continuing. "Henry, I was thinking about how much luckier he is than you and I will ever be."

He pointed to the third person by thrusting his thumb downward toward the box they were sitting on.

"You and me, Henry, when we die, we'll be lucky if we get enough stones over our bodies to keep the dogs away from us."

"But we don't have people and money and all the rest, like him," Henry replied. "Long-distance funerals are something you and I can't exactly afford."

"What bothers me, Henry, is why someone like this guy, who's a lord or something back in his own country and has never had to worry about food or shelter, comes wandering around to these godforsaken corners of the world—that's what I can't quite understand."

"He could have lived to a ripe old age if he had stayed at home," Henry agreed.

Bill opened his mouth to say something, but thought better of it. Instead, he gestured toward the wall of darkness that surrounded them on all sides. The complete blackness revealed no hint of shape or form; only a pair of eyes could be seen glowing like burning embers. Henry nodded toward a second pair, then a third. A ring of these glowing eyes had formed around their campsite. Every so often, a pair of eyes would shift position, or vanish only to reappear moments later.

The dogs' agitation had been growing stronger, and they rushed in a wave of sudden terror to the side of the fire closest to them, cowering and crawling around the men's legs. During the chaos, one of the dogs had been knocked over at the fire's edge, and it cried out in pain and alarm as the scent of its burned fur filled the air. The disturbance made the ring of eyes move uneasily for a moment and even pull back slightly, but they settled back into place once the dogs grew calm again.

"Henry, it's a terrible misfortune to be out of ammunition."

Bill had finished smoking his pipe and was helping his companion spread the bed made of fur and blankets on top of the spruce branches he had arranged over the snow before dinner. Henry made a grunting sound and started untying his moccasins.

"How many cartridges did you say you had left?" he asked.

"Three," came the answer. "And I wish it was three hundred. Then I'd show them what for, damn them!"

He angrily shook his fist at the glowing eyes and started

carefully positioning his moccasins in front of the fire.

"And I wish this cold snap would break," he continued. "It's been fifty below for two weeks now. And I wish I'd never started on this trip, Henry. I don't like the looks of it. I don't feel right, somehow. And while I'm wishing, I wish the trip was over and done with, and you and me sitting by the fire in Fort McGurry just about now and playing cribbage—that's what I wish."

Henry grunted and climbed into bed. As he was falling asleep, he was awakened by his companion's voice.

"Tell me, Henry, that other creature that came in and caught a fish—why didn't the dogs attack it? That's what's troubling me."

"You're worrying too much, Bill," came the sleepy response. "You were never like this before. Just shut up now and go to sleep, and you'll be perfectly fine in the morning. Your stomach is upset, that's what's bothering you."

The men slept heavily, breathing deeply as they lay side by side beneath their shared blanket. The fire gradually burned down, and the glowing eyes moved closer, tightening the circle they had formed around the campsite. The dogs huddled together in terror, occasionally growling threateningly when a pair of eyes came too near. At one point their commotion grew so loud that it woke Bill. He carefully climbed out of bed, taking care not to wake his sleeping partner, and added more wood to the fire. As the flames began to rise again, the circle of eyes retreated farther into the darkness. He looked casually at the clustered dogs. He rubbed his eyes and examined them more carefully. Then he crawled back under the blankets.

"Henry," he said. "Oh, Henry."

Henry groaned as he woke up and asked, "What's the problem now?"

"Nothing," came the answer; "it's just that there are seven of them again. I just counted."

Henry acknowledged receiving the information with a grunt

that turned into a snore as he fell back asleep.

In the morning, Henry was the first to wake up and got his companion out of bed. Dawn was still three hours away, even though it was already six o'clock; and in the darkness, Henry busied himself preparing breakfast, while Bill rolled up the blankets and got the sled ready for loading.

"Tell me, Henry," he asked suddenly, "how many dogs did you say we had?"

"Six."

"Wrong," Bill declared with triumph.

"Seven again?" Henry asked.

"No, five; one's gone."

"What the hell!" Henry shouted angrily, abandoning his cooking to come over and count the dogs.

"You're right, Bill," he concluded. "Fatty's gone."

"And he moved incredibly fast once he got going. You couldn't have seen him through all the dust he kicked up."

"No chance at all," Henry concluded. "They just swallowed him alive. I bet he was yelping as he went down their throats, damn them!"

"He was always a foolish dog," said Bill.

"But no foolish dog should be stupid enough to run off and kill itself like that." He examined the rest of the team with a calculating gaze that quickly assessed the key characteristics of each animal. "I'm certain none of the others would do such a thing."

"You couldn't drive them away from the fire with a club," Bill agreed. "I always thought there was something wrong with Fatty anyway."

And this served as the epitaph for a dead dog on the Northland trail—more generous than the epitaphs given to many other dogs, and to many men as well.

Chapter II: The She-Wolf

After finishing breakfast and securing their minimal camping gear to the sled, the men turned away from the warm fire and headed out into the darkness. Immediately, haunting cries began to echo through the air—wild, melancholy sounds that called out through the darkness and bitter cold, answering one another across the vast emptiness. All conversation stopped. Daylight finally arrived at nine o'clock. By noon, the southern sky took on a rosy glow, marking the spot where the curve of the earth blocked the sun from reaching this northern wilderness. But the pink light quickly disappeared. The dim gray daylight that lingered lasted only until three o'clock, when it too vanished, and the heavy blanket of Arctic night settled over the desolate and silent landscape.

As night fell, the hunting calls from the right, left, and behind grew nearer—so near that they repeatedly sent waves of terror through the struggling dogs, causing them to panic briefly.

At the end of one such panic, when he and Henry had gotten the dogs back in their harnesses, Bill said:

"I wish they would find what they're looking for somewhere else and go away and leave us alone."

"They really get on your nerves terribly," Henry agreed sympathetically.

They didn't speak again until they had set up camp.

Henry was leaning over and adding ice to the bubbling pot of beans when he was startled by the sound of a strike, a shout from Bill, and a sharp growling cry of pain from the dogs. He stood up straight just in time to see a shadowy figure vanishing across the snow into the darkness. Then he spotted Bill, standing among the dogs, looking both victorious and disappointed, holding a heavy stick in one hand and the tail and part of a dried salmon in the other.

"It got half of it," he announced; "but I got a hit on it just the same. Do you hear it squeal?"

"What did it look like?" Henry asked.

"I couldn't see clearly. But it had four legs and a mouth and hair and looked like any dog."

"Must be a tame wolf, I reckon."

"It's incredibly tame, whatever it is, coming in here at feeding time and getting its share of fish."

That night, after they finished supper and sat on the rectangular box smoking their pipes, the circle of glowing eyes moved in even closer than before.

"I wish a bunch of moose or something would show up and they'd go away and leave us alone," Bill said.

Henry grunted with a tone that wasn't entirely sympathetic, and for fifteen minutes they continued sitting in silence, Henry gazing at the fire while Bill watched the circle of glowing eyes that gleamed in the darkness just outside the reach of the firelight.

"I wish we were pulling into McGurry right now," he began again.

"Stop your complaining and grumbling," Henry exploded angrily. "You've got an upset stomach. That's what's wrong with you. Take a spoonful of baking soda, and you'll feel much better and be more pleasant to be around."

In the morning Henry was awakened by intense cursing that came from Bill's mouth. Henry pushed himself up on his elbow and saw his companion standing among the dogs next to the restocked fire, his arms raised in angry protest, his face twisted with rage.

"Hello!" Henry called out. "What's going on now?"

"The frog is gone," came the answer.

"No."

"I tell you yes."

Henry jumped out of his blankets and rushed to the dogs. He counted them carefully, then joined his partner in cursing the wilderness that had taken another dog from them.

"Frog was the strongest dog of the group," Bill declared at last.

"And he wasn't a foolish dog either," Henry added.

And so the second epitaph in two days was recorded.

A somber breakfast was consumed, and the four surviving dogs were hitched to the sled. The day mirrored those that had come before. The men labored in silence across the surface of the frozen landscape. The quiet remained uninterrupted except for the calls of their hunters, who, though invisible, stayed close behind them. As night fell in the middle of the afternoon, the calls grew nearer as the pursuers closed in following their usual pattern; and the dogs became agitated and scared, succumbing to fits of terror that snarled the harness lines and further discouraged the two men.

"There, that should take care of you foolish creatures," Bill said with satisfaction that night, standing upright after finishing his work.

Henry stopped cooking and came over to take a look. His partner hadn't just tied up the dogs—he had secured them using the Indian method with sticks. Around each dog's neck, he had wrapped a leather strap. He then attached a sturdy stick, four or five feet long, to this strap, positioning it so close to the neck that the dog couldn't reach it with its teeth. The opposite end of the stick was secured to a ground stake with another leather strap. This setup made it impossible for the dog to chew through the leather on its end of the stick. Meanwhile, the stick itself kept the dog from reaching the leather that held the other end in place.

Henry nodded in approval.

"It's the only device that will ever contain One Ear," he said. "He can chew through leather as cleanly as a knife and just about half as fast. They'll all be here in the morning safe and sound."

"You can bet they will," Bill confirmed. "If one of them turns up missing, I'll go without my coffee."

"They just know we're not armed to kill," Henry said at bedtime, pointing to the gleaming circle that surrounded them. "If we could fire a couple of shots at them, they'd show more respect. They get closer every night. Block the firelight from your eyes and look carefully—there! Did you see that one?"

For a while, the two men entertained themselves by observing the shifting shadows of unclear shapes at the border of the fire's glow. When they focused intently and kept their gaze fixed on spots where pairs of eyes glowed in the darkness, the outline of each creature would gradually become visible. They could occasionally watch these figures moving about.

A noise from the dogs caught the men's attention. One Ear was making sharp, excited whimpers, straining against his tether toward the darkness, and stopping occasionally to frantically bite at the stick with his teeth.

"Look at that, Bill," Henry whispered.

A dog-like creature slipped into the firelight with a sneaky, sideways movement. It moved with a mixture of suspicion and boldness, carefully watching the men while keeping its attention focused on the dogs. One Ear stretched as far as the stick would allow toward the newcomer and whined with excitement.

"That fool One Ear doesn't seem very scared," Bill said quietly.

"It's a female wolf," Henry whispered back, "and that explains what happened to Fatty and Frog. She's the bait for the pack. She lures out the dog and then all the others attack and devour him."

The fire crackled. A log broke apart with a loud sputtering sound. When it heard this noise, the strange creature jumped back into the darkness.

"Henry, I'm thinking," Bill announced.

"Thinking what?"

"I think that was the one I beat with the club."

"There isn't the slightest doubt in the world," was Henry's response.

"And right here I want to point out," Bill continued, "that that animal's familiarity with campfires is suspicious and immoral."

"It definitely knows more than any self-respecting wolf should know," Henry agreed. "A wolf that's smart enough to show up with the dogs at feeding time has been through some experiences."

"Old Villan once had a dog that ran away with the wolves," Bill thinks out loud. "I should know. I shot it out of the pack in a moose pasture over on Little Stick. And Old Villan cried like a baby. He said he hadn't seen it for three years. It had been with the wolves all that time."

"I think you're right, Bill. That wolf is actually a dog, and it's been fed fish by hand from humans many times before."

"And if I get a chance at it, that wolf that's a dog will just be meat," Bill declared. "We can't afford to lose any more animals."

"But you only have three cartridges," Henry objected.

"I'll wait for a guaranteed opportunity," was the response.

In the morning, Henry rekindled the fire and prepared breakfast while his partner continued snoring loudly nearby.

"You were sleeping far too comfortably," Henry told him as he woke him up for breakfast. "I didn't have the heart to wake you."

Bill started eating drowsily. He saw that his cup was empty and began reaching for the pot. However, the pot was too far away and sat next to Henry.

"Say, Henry," he gently scolded, "haven't you forgotten something?"

Henry looked around very carefully and shook his head. Bill held up the empty cup.

"You don't get any coffee," Henry announced.

"Haven't we run out?" Bill asked anxiously.

"Nope."

"Don't you think it will hurt my digestion?"

"Nope."

A wave of angry blood rushed to Bill's face, turning it red.

"Then I'm just feeling warm and anxious to hear you explain yourself," he said.

"Spanker's gone," Henry replied.

Without rushing, looking like someone who had accepted his bad luck, Bill turned his head and counted the dogs from where he was sitting.

"How did it happen?" he asked without emotion.

Henry shrugged his shoulders. "I don't know. Unless One Ear chewed them loose. He couldn't have done it himself, that's for sure."

"That damn dog." Bill spoke seriously and deliberately, showing no sign of the fury burning inside him. "Just because he couldn't chew himself free, he goes and chews Spanker loose."

"Well, Spanker's troubles are over anyway; I guess he's been digested by now and is scattered across the landscape in the bellies of twenty different wolves," was Henry's epitaph for this, the latest lost dog. "Have some coffee, Bill."

But Bill shook his head.

"Go on," Henry pleaded, raising the pot.

Bill pushed his cup away. "I'll be damned if I do. I said I wouldn't if any dog went missing, and I won't."

"It's really good coffee," Henry said enticingly.

But Bill was stubborn, and he ate a dry breakfast washed down with mumbled curses at One Ear for the trick he had played.

"I'll tie them up out of reach of each other tonight," Bill said as they took the trail.

They had traveled just over a hundred yards when Henry, who was leading the way, bent down and picked up something his snowshoe had bumped into. It was too dark to see what it was, but he could tell what it was by feeling it. He threw it back so that it hit the sled and bounced along until it came to rest on Bill's snowshoes.

"Maybe you'll need that in your business," Henry said.

Bill let out a cry. All that remained of Spanker was the stick he had been tied to.

"They ate everything, hide and all," Bill announced. "The stick is as clean as a whistle. They've eaten the leather off both ends. They're incredibly hungry, Henry, and they'll have you and me worried before this trip is over."

Henry laughed defiantly. "I haven't been followed like this by wolves before, but I've been through much worse and stayed healthy. It takes more than a handful of those troublesome creatures to finish me off, Bill, my friend."

"I don't know, I don't know," Bill muttered with a sense of foreboding.

"Well, you'll know for sure when we arrive in McGurry."

"I'm not feeling particularly enthusiastic," Bill persisted.

"You don't look well, that's what's wrong with you," Henry declared with authority. "What you need is quinine, and I'm going to give you a strong dose as soon as we reach McGurry."

Bill grunted to show he disagreed with the diagnosis, then fell silent. The day was just like every other day. Light appeared at nine o'clock. At noon, the southern horizon grew warm from the hidden sun, and then the cold gray of afternoon began, which would blend into night three hours later.

It was right after the sun made its weak attempt to show itself that Bill pulled the rifle out from under the sled ropes and said:

"You keep going, Henry, I'm going to see what I can find out."

"You should stay with the sled," his partner objected. "You only have three bullets left, and there's no telling what could happen."

"Who's croaking now?" Bill asked triumphantly.

Henry didn't respond and continued trudging forward by himself, though he frequently looked back with worry into the gray emptiness where his companion had vanished. An hour later, using the shortcuts that the sled couldn't navigate, Bill caught up.

"They're spread out and moving along a wide area," he said. "They're keeping pace with us while hunting for prey at the same time. You see, they're confident they have us, but they know they need to wait for the right moment to get us. Meanwhile, they're happy to grab anything edible that comes their way."

"You mean they think they have us figured out," Henry objected sharply.

But Bill ignored him. "I've seen some of them. They're extremely thin. They haven't had a bite to eat in weeks, I figure, except for Fatty and Frog and Spanker, and there are so many of them that those meals didn't go very far. They're remarkably skinny. Their ribs look like washboards, and their stomachs are pressed right up against their spines. They're pretty desperate, I can tell you. They'll be going crazy soon, and then we'd better watch out."

A few minutes later, Henry, who was now traveling behind the sled, let out a low, warning whistle. Bill turned and looked, then quietly stopped the dogs. Behind them, coming around the last bend and clearly visible on the very trail they had just traveled, a furry, sneaking figure trotted forward. Its nose stayed close to the trail, and it moved with an unusual, smooth, effortless stride. When they stopped, it stopped too, lifting its head and watching them steadily with nostrils that twitched as it picked up and analyzed their scent.

"It's the she-wolf," Bill answered.

The dogs had settled down in the snow, and he walked past them to join his partner in the sled. Together they watched the strange creature that had been following them for days and had already managed to destroy half of their dog team.

After carefully examining them, the animal moved forward a few steps. It did this several times until it was about a hundred yards away. The creature stopped with its head raised, standing near a cluster of spruce trees, using both its eyes and nose to study the group of men who were watching it. The animal gazed at them with a strange longing, similar to how a dog might look, but this longing contained none of a dog's affection. This was a yearning born from hunger, as cruel as its own teeth, as ruthless as the freezing cold itself.

It was enormous for a wolf, with its lean body showing the features of an animal that ranked among the biggest of its species.

"Stands pretty close to two and a half feet at the shoulders," Henry commented. "And I'll bet it isn't far from five feet long."

"That's a pretty unusual color for a wolf," Bill observed. "I've never seen a red wolf before. It looks almost cinnamon-colored to me."

The animal definitely wasn't cinnamon-colored. Its fur was genuine wolf fur. The main color was gray, but it had a subtle reddish tint—a puzzling shade that came and went, more like a trick of the eye, sometimes clearly gray, and other times showing traces and flashes of an unclear reddish color that couldn't be described using normal experience.

"It looks exactly like a big husky sled dog," Bill said. "I wouldn't be surprised to see it wag its tail."

"Hello, you husky!" he called out. "Come here, whatever your name is."

"I'm not scared of you at all," Henry laughed.

Bill waved his hand at it in a threatening manner and yelled loudly, but the creature showed no signs of fear. The only difference they could observe was that it became more alert. It continued to watch them with the ruthless longing of hunger. They represented food, and it was starving; it wanted to approach and devour them if it had the courage.

"Listen, Henry," Bill said, instinctively dropping his voice to a whisper because of what he was copying. "We have three cartridges. But it's a sure shot. We couldn't miss it. It has taken three of our dogs, and we should put an end to it. What do you think?"

Henry nodded in agreement. Bill carefully pulled the gun out from beneath the sled ropes. He was raising the weapon toward his shoulder, but he never completed the motion. At that exact moment, the female wolf jumped sideways off the path into a cluster of spruce trees and vanished from sight.

The two men looked at each other. Henry let out a long, knowing whistle.

"I should have known it," Bill scolded himself out loud as he put the gun back. "Obviously a wolf that's smart enough to come in with the dogs at feeding time would know all about guns. I'm telling you right now, Henry, that animal is the reason for all our problems. We'd have six dogs right now instead of three if it weren't for her. And I'm telling you right now, Henry, I'm going to get her. She's too clever to be shot out in the open. But I'm going to wait for her. I'll ambush her as sure as my name is Bill."

"You don't need to go too far when you do it," his partner warned. "If that pack decides to attack you, those three cartridges won't be worth more than three shouts in hell. Those animals are extremely hungry, and once they begin their assault, they'll definitely get you, Bill."

They set up camp early that evening. Three dogs couldn't pull the sled as quickly or for as many hours as six dogs could, and they were clearly showing signs of exhaustion. The men went to bed early, with Bill first making sure the dogs were tied up far enough apart so they couldn't bite each other.

The wolves were becoming increasingly bold, and the men found themselves waking up from sleep multiple times. The wolves came so close that the dogs became wild with fear, and it became necessary to add more wood to the fire periodically to keep these daring intruders at a safer distance.

"I've heard sailors talk about sharks following a ship," Bill said, as he crawled back into the blankets after refueling the fire. "Well, those wolves are land sharks. They know their business better than we do, and they're not following our trail like this for their health. They're going to get us. They're definitely going to get us, Henry."

"They've already got you halfway, talking like that," Henry shot back sharply. "A man is half defeated when he admits he is. And you're half consumed from the way you're carrying on about it."

"They've gotten away with better men than you and me," Bill replied.

"Oh, shut up your complaining. You make me completely exhausted."

Henry rolled over angrily on his side, but he was surprised that Bill didn't show any similar burst of anger. This wasn't like Bill at all, since he usually got upset easily when someone spoke harshly to him. Henry thought about this for a long time before falling asleep, and as his eyelids grew heavy and he drifted off, his final thought was: "There's no mistaking it, Bill's really down in the dumps. I'll need to cheer him up tomorrow."

Chapter III: The Hunger Cry

The day started off well. They hadn't lost any dogs overnight, and they set out on the trail into the quiet, dark, and cold with relatively good spirits. Bill appeared to have forgotten his worries from the night before, and he even became playful with the dogs when they tipped over the sled on a rough section of trail at midday.

It was an awkward mix-up. The sled had flipped over and gotten stuck between a tree trunk and a massive boulder, forcing them to unhitch the dogs to sort out the mess. Both men were hunched over the sled, working to turn it right-side up, when Henry noticed One Ear sneaking away.

"Hey, you, One Ear!" he shouted, standing up straight and spinning around to face the dog.

But One Ear started running across the snow, his harness straps dragging behind him. There, in the snow along their previous path, the female wolf was waiting for him. As he got closer to her, he suddenly became careful. He slowed to a watchful and careful walk before stopping completely. He looked at her with both wariness and longing. She appeared to smile at him, baring her teeth in a friendly way rather than threatening. She took a few playful steps toward him, then stopped. One Ear approached her, remaining alert and cautious, his tail and ears upright, his head held high.

He attempted to touch noses with her, but she pulled back in a playful and shy manner. Each time he moved forward, she moved backward in response. Gradually, she was drawing him away from the safety of being near his human companions. At one moment, as if some unclear warning had passed through his mind, he turned around and glanced back at the upturned sled, at his fellow dogs, and at the two men who were shouting to him.

But whatever thought was taking shape in his mind was scattered by the she-wolf, who moved toward him, touched noses with him for a brief moment, and then continued her playful withdrawal as he pursued her once again.

In the meantime, Bill had remembered the rifle. However, it was trapped under the overturned sled, and by the time Henry had helped him set the load upright, One Ear and the she-wolf were too close to each other and the distance was too far to risk taking a shot.

Too late, One Ear realized his error. Before they could see what was causing it, the two men watched him turn around and begin running back in their direction. Then, coming at a right angle to the trail and blocking his escape route, they spotted a dozen wolves—lean and gray—leaping across the snow. In that instant, the she-wolf's coy and playful behavior vanished. With a growl, she lunged at One Ear. He pushed her away with his shoulder, and with his escape path blocked but still determined to reach the sled, he changed direction to try circling around to it. More wolves kept appearing and joining the pursuit. The she-wolf stayed one jump behind One Ear, keeping pace with him.

"Where are you going?" Henry suddenly demanded, placing his hand on his partner's arm.

Bill shook it off. "I won't stand for it," he said. "They're not going to get any more of our dogs if I can help it."

Gun in hand, he dove into the thick brush that bordered the trail. His plan was clear. Using the sled as the center point of the circle that One Ear was running, Bill intended to intercept that circle at a spot ahead of the chase. With his rifle and the bright daylight on his side, he might be able to intimidate the wolves and rescue the dog.

"Hey, Bill!" Henry shouted after him. "Be careful! Don't take any chances!"

Henry settled onto the sled and observed the scene unfolding before him. There wasn't anything else he could do. Bill had already disappeared from view, but occasionally, appearing and vanishing among the thick brush and scattered clusters of spruce trees, One Ear could be spotted. Henry concluded that the situation was without hope. The dog was fully aware of the peril it faced, yet it was racing along the outer perimeter while the wolf pack pursued along the inner and more direct route. It was futile to imagine that One Ear could outrun his hunters enough to cut across their path ahead of them and make it back to the sled.

The different paths were quickly converging toward a single point. Somewhere out there in the snow, hidden from his view by trees and dense brush, Henry knew that the wolf pack, One Ear, and Bill were about to meet. It all happened much too fast, far faster than he had anticipated. He heard a gunshot, then two more shots fired in quick succession, and he realized that Bill had run out of ammunition. Then he heard a tremendous eruption of snarls and yelps. He recognized One Ear's cry of pain and fear, and he heard a wolf's howl that indicated a wounded animal. And that was everything. The snarling stopped. The yelping faded away. Silence descended once more over the desolate wilderness.

He sat on the sled for a long time. There was no need for him to go and see what had happened. He knew it as if it had taken place right in front of him. At one point, he suddenly stirred and quickly pulled the axe out from under the ropes. But he continued to sit there thinking for quite a while longer, with the two remaining dogs crouched and shaking at his feet.

At last he got up in a tired way, as if all the strength had drained from his body, and began to harness the dogs to the sled. He put a rope over his shoulder, a man-trace, and pulled alongside the dogs. He didn't travel far. At the first sign of darkness he hurried to set up camp, and he made sure he had plenty of firewood. He fed the dogs, cooked and ate his dinner, and made his bed near the fire.

But he wasn't meant to enjoy that bed. Before he could close his eyes, the wolves had come too close for comfort. He no longer had to strain his eyes to see them. They surrounded him and the fire in a tight circle, and he could clearly make them out in the flickering light as they lay down, sat up, crawled forward on their stomachs, or moved back and forth. Some of them were even sleeping. Here and there he spotted one curled up in the snow like a dog, getting the rest that he himself was now denied.

He maintained the fire at a bright blaze, understanding that it was the only barrier standing between his flesh and their ravenous teeth. His two dogs remained close beside him, positioned on each side, pressing against him for safety, whining and whimpering, and occasionally growling fiercely when a wolf ventured closer than normal. During these instances, when his dogs growled, the entire circle would become restless, the wolves rising to their feet and cautiously pushing forward, a symphony of growls and anxious barks echoing around him. Then the circle would settle down once more, and scattered wolves would return to their interrupted sleep.

But this circle kept steadily closing in on him. Little by little, one step at a time, with a wolf creeping forward here and another wolf creeping forward there, the circle grew smaller until the beasts were nearly close enough to leap. Then he would grab burning sticks from the fire and throw them at the pack. This always caused them to quickly retreat, along with angry howls and scared growls when a well-thrown stick hit and burned an overly bold animal.

Morning arrived to find the man exhausted and weathered, his eyes wide open from lack of sleep. He prepared breakfast in the dark, and at nine o'clock, when daylight came and the wolf pack retreated, he began the work he had thought through during the long nighttime hours. He cut down young saplings and turned them into crossbeams for a scaffold by tying them high up on the trunks of standing trees. He used the sled rope as a lifting line, and with the dogs' help, he raised the coffin to the top of the scaffold.

"They got Bill, and they might get me, but they'll never get you, young man," he said, speaking to the dead body in its tree tomb.

Then he started down the trail, the lighter sled bouncing along behind the eager dogs; they also understood that safety awaited them once they reached Fort McGurry. The wolves had become bolder in their chase, trotting calmly behind and spreading out on both sides, their red tongues hanging out, their thin flanks revealing the rippling ribs with each step. They were extremely thin, nothing more than skin stretched over skeletal frames, with stringy muscles—so emaciated that Henry couldn't help but wonder how they managed to stay on their feet without collapsing right there in the snow.

He didn't dare to travel until darkness fell. At noon, the sun not only warmed the southern horizon, but its pale, golden upper edge actually appeared above the skyline. He took this as a positive sign. The days were getting longer. The sun was coming back. But as soon as the cheerful light faded, he made camp. Several hours of gray daylight and dark twilight remained, and he used this time to chop a massive supply of firewood.

With nightfall came terror. The starving wolves were becoming increasingly bold, and Henry's lack of sleep was taking its toll. Despite his efforts to stay alert, he found himself nodding off while crouched beside the fire, wrapped in blankets with the axe resting between his knees and a dog pressed tightly against each side of his body. He woke up at one point to find a massive gray wolf standing directly in front of him, less than twelve feet away—one of the largest members of the pack. As Henry watched, the creature casually stretched its body like a lazy dog, yawned openly in his direction, and stared at him with an ownership in its eyes, as though Henry was nothing more than a postponed meal that would soon be devoured.

This certainty was displayed by the entire pack. He could count at least twenty of them, gazing at him with hunger or peacefully resting in the snow. They brought to mind children sitting around a dinner table, waiting for permission to start eating. And he was their meal! He wondered how and when they would begin to feast.

As he stacked wood on the fire, he developed a newfound appreciation for his own body that he had never experienced before. He observed his moving muscles and became fascinated by the intricate workings of his fingers. In the firelight, he bent his fingers slowly and repeatedly, sometimes one at a time, sometimes all together, stretching them wide or making quick grasping motions. He examined how his nails were formed and poked his fingertips, sometimes sharply and other times gently, measuring the nerve responses they created. This captivated him, and he suddenly grew fond of this remarkable flesh of his that functioned so beautifully, smoothly, and precisely. Then he would glance fearfully at the circle of wolves waiting expectantly around him, and the realization would hit him like a physical blow that this amazing body of his, this living flesh, was nothing more than meat, prey for starving animals, to be ripped apart and shredded by their ravenous fangs, to nourish them just as the moose and rabbit had so often nourished him.

He woke from a half-sleep filled with nightmares to find the reddish she-wolf sitting right in front of him. She was no more than six feet away, positioned in the snow and gazing at him with longing. The two dogs at his feet were whimpering and growling, but she paid them no attention. Her focus was entirely on the man, and he stared back at her for several moments. She showed no signs of aggression or threat. Her expression held only deep yearning, though he understood this longing stemmed from an equally intense hunger. He represented her next meal, and seeing him triggered her appetite. Her mouth fell open, saliva began to drip, and she licked her lips in eager anticipation.

A wave of terror shot through him. He quickly reached for a burning stick to hurl at her. But even as he grabbed for it, before his fingers could grasp the weapon, she leaped back to safety; and he realized she was accustomed to having objects thrown at her. She had growled as she jumped away, exposing her white fangs down to their roots, all her longing disappearing, replaced by a predatory hatred that made him tremble. He looked at the hand holding the burning stick, observing the skillful delicacy of the fingers gripping it, how they adapted to every uneven part of the surface, wrapping over and under and around the rough wood, and one small finger, positioned too near the flaming end of the stick, instinctively and automatically pulling back from the painful heat to find a cooler place to hold; and at that same moment he seemed to envision those same responsive and delicate fingers being crushed and mangled by the white teeth of the she-wolf. He had never cherished this body of his as much as he did now when his hold on it was so uncertain.

Throughout the entire night, he used flaming torches to keep the ravenous pack at bay. Whenever he fell asleep against his will, the whining and growling of the animals woke him up. Dawn arrived, but this was the first time that daylight didn't drive the wolves away. The man waited uselessly for them to leave. They stayed in a ring around him and his fire, showing a bold sense of ownership that undermined the confidence that morning light had given him.

He made one final, desperate effort to escape onto the trail. However, the instant he stepped away from the fire's protection, the most aggressive wolf lunged at him, though it fell just short of its target. He managed to save himself by jumping backward, with the wolf's jaws snapping shut barely six inches from his leg. The remaining members of the pack had now risen and were rushing toward him, forcing him to hurl burning sticks in all directions to push them back to a safe distance.

Even during daylight hours, he didn't dare venture away from the fire to cut fresh wood. A massive dead spruce stood towering just twenty feet away. He spent half the day stretching his campfire toward the tree, keeping a half dozen burning sticks ready at all times to throw at his enemies. Once he reached the tree, he examined the surrounding forest to determine the best direction to fell it for maximum firewood.

The night was just like the one before, except that his need for sleep was becoming overwhelming. The growling of his dogs was losing its effectiveness. Moreover, they were growling constantly, and his numb and sleepy senses no longer noticed the changes in tone and strength. He woke up suddenly. The female wolf was less than three feet away from him. Automatically, at close range, without releasing his grip on it, he shoved a burning stick directly into her open and snarling mouth. She jumped back, howling in pain, and while he enjoyed the scent of burning flesh and fur, he watched her shake her head and growl angrily about twenty feet away.

This time, before falling asleep again, he secured a burning piece of pine to his right hand. His eyes had been shut for only a few minutes when the searing flame against his skin woke him up. He stuck to this routine for several hours. Each time the fire roused him, he chased away the wolves with flaming branches, built up the fire again, and repositioned the pine torch on his hand. Everything went smoothly, but eventually there came a moment when he didn't attach the pine torch securely enough. As his eyelids closed, it slipped from his grasp.

He dreamed. It felt like he was at Fort McGurry. The place was warm and cozy, and he was playing cribbage with the Factor. It also seemed like the fort was under siege by wolves. They were howling right at the gates, and occasionally he and the Factor would stop their game to listen and chuckle at the wolves' useless attempts to break in. Then, in the strange way dreams unfold, there was a loud crash. The door burst wide open. He could see wolves pouring into the fort's large living room. They were jumping straight toward him and the Factor. When the door exploded open, their howling became incredibly loud. This howling was now disturbing him. His dream was shifting into something else—he couldn't tell what; but throughout it all, following him everywhere, the howling continued.

And then he woke up to discover the howling was real. There was tremendous snarling and yelping. The wolves were charging at him. They surrounded him completely. One wolf's teeth had clamped down on his arm. Without thinking, he jumped into the fire, and as he jumped, he felt the sharp cut of teeth ripping through the flesh of his leg. Then a fire fight began. His thick mittens gave his hands temporary protection, and he threw burning coals through the air in every direction, until the campfire looked like a volcano.

But this couldn't continue much longer. The intense heat was causing blisters to form on his face, his eyebrows and eyelashes had been burned away, and the scorching temperature was becoming too much for his feet to bear. Holding a blazing stick in each hand, he jumped to the fire's edge. The wolves had been forced to retreat. All around him, wherever the glowing embers had landed, the snow was hissing and steaming, and every so often a withdrawing wolf would leap wildly and snort and growl, signaling that it had stepped on one of these burning coals.

Throwing his burning sticks at the closest enemies, the man shoved his smoking mittens into the snow and stomped around to cool his feet. His two dogs were gone, and he understood clearly that they had become part of the extended meal that had started days earlier with Fatty, and he would probably be the final course in the days ahead.

"You haven't caught me yet!" he shouted, angrily shaking his fist at the starving animals; and when they heard his voice the entire circle became restless, there was a collective growl, and the female wolf moved closer to him across the snow and observed him with ravenous longing.

He began working on a fresh idea that had occurred to him. He expanded the fire into a wide circle. Within this circle he crouched down, placing his sleeping gear beneath him as protection from the melting snow. Once he had vanished inside his barrier of flames, the entire pack approached the fire's edge with curiosity to discover what had happened to him. Until now they had been kept away from the fire, and they now gathered in a tight circle, resembling a group of dogs, blinking and yawning and stretching their thin bodies in the unusual warmth. Then the she-wolf settled down, lifted her nose toward a star, and started to howl. One after another the wolves joined in with her, until the entire pack, sitting on their haunches with noses pointing toward the sky, was howling their cry of hunger.

Dawn arrived, bringing daylight with it. The fire was burning low. The fuel had been exhausted, and more was needed. The man tried to step outside his circle of flames, but the wolves rushed forward to confront him. Flaming sticks forced them to jump away, but they no longer retreated afterward. He struggled in vain to push them back. When he gave up and staggered back inside his circle, a wolf lunged at him, missed its target, and landed with all four paws in the hot coals. It howled in terror while simultaneously growling, then scrambled backward to cool its burned paws in the snow.

The man settled onto his blankets in a crouched position. He leaned forward from his waist. His shoulders hung loose and slack, and with his head resting on his knees, he clearly showed that he had abandoned the fight. From time to time he lifted his head to observe the fire dying out. The ring of flames and glowing embers was splitting apart into separate pieces with gaps forming between them. These gaps widened while the remaining sections grew smaller.

"I suppose you can come and get me whenever you want," he mumbled. "Either way, I'm going to sleep."

Once he woke up, he noticed a gap in the circle directly ahead of him, and through that opening, he could see the she-wolf staring at him.

Once more he woke up, a short while later, though it felt like hours had passed. A strange transformation had occurred—so strange that it jolted him completely awake. Something had changed. At first, he couldn't grasp what it was. Then he figured it out. The wolves had disappeared. Only the packed-down snow remained as evidence of how close they had come to him. Sleep was rising up and taking hold of him once more, his head was dropping toward his knees, when he suddenly snapped alert.

There were shouts from the men, the grinding noise of sleds, the groaning of leather harnesses, and the excited whining of dogs pulling hard against their traces. Four sleds came up from the riverbed into the camp nestled among the trees. About six men gathered around the figure who was hunched over the fading fire. They shook him and poked at him, trying to bring him back to awareness. He stared at them with the glazed look of someone intoxicated and mumbled incoherently in a drowsy, confused voice.

"Red she-wolf. . . . Come in with the dogs at feeding time. . . . First she ate the dog food. . . . Then she ate the dogs. . . . And after that she ate Bill. . . . "

"Where's Lord Alfred?" one of the men shouted in his ear, shaking him violently.

He slowly shook his head. "No, she didn't eat him. . . . He's perched in a tree back at the last camp."

"Dead?" the man shouted.

"And in a box," Henry answered. He jerked his shoulder irritably away from the grip of his questioner. "Listen, leave me alone. . . . I'm just completely exhausted. . . . Good night, everybody."

His eyes flickered and closed. His chin dropped forward onto his chest. And even as they gently lowered him onto the blankets, his snores were already echoing in the cold air.

But there was another sound. Far away and barely audible in the distant wilderness, the howling of the starving wolf pack echoed as it picked up the scent trail of different prey than the man who had just escaped them.

Part II

Chapter I: The Battle of The Fangs

The female wolf was the first to hear the sound of human voices and the whimpering of the sled dogs, and she was also the first to leap away from the trapped man surrounded by his circle of fading fire. The pack had been reluctant to abandon the prey they had tracked down, and they waited for several minutes, confirming what they were hearing, before they too bounded away following the path the female wolf had taken.

Leading the pack was a massive gray wolf—one of its primary leaders. He was the one who guided the pack's path as they pursued the female wolf. He was the one who growled threateningly at the younger pack members or snapped at them with his teeth when they boldly attempted to overtake him. And he was the one who quickened the pace when he spotted the she-wolf, now moving slowly through the snow.

She fell into step beside him as if that were her natural place and matched the rhythm of the pack. He didn't growl at her or bare his teeth when she happened to surge ahead of him during their run. Instead, he appeared well-disposed toward her—perhaps too much so for her liking, since he tended to run close beside her, and whenever he came too near, she was the one who snarled and bared her teeth. She didn't hesitate to give his shoulder a sharp bite when the moment called for it. During these instances, he showed no signs of anger. He simply leaped to one side and ran stiffly forward for several clumsy bounds, his posture and behavior resembling that of an embarrassed young man from the countryside.

This was his only problem when running with the pack, but she faced additional challenges. On her other side ran a lean old wolf, gray-haired and bearing scars from countless fights. He always ran on her right side. The fact that he had only one eye, the left one, might explain this positioning. He was also prone to crowding her, swerving toward her until his scarred snout touched her body, shoulder, or neck. Just like with the running mate on her left, she fought off these advances with her teeth, but when both wolves pursued her attention simultaneously, she was roughly pushed around, forced to snap quickly at either side to drive both suitors away while maintaining her forward momentum with the pack and watching where she placed her feet. During these moments, her running companions bared their teeth and growled menacingly at each other. They could have fought, but even courtship and its competition took second place to the pack's more urgent need for food.

After each rejection, when the old wolf suddenly veered away from the sharp-toothed target of his longing, he bumped into a young three-year-old that ran on his blind right side. This young wolf had reached his full size; and, given the weak and starving state of the pack, he had more than the usual energy and spirit. Even so, he ran with his head level with the shoulder of his one-eyed elder. When he dared to run alongside the older wolf (which was rare), a growl and a snap forced him back to the shoulder position again. Sometimes, though, he carefully and slowly fell behind and squeezed in between the old leader and the she-wolf. This was doubly unwelcome, even triply unwelcome. When she growled her annoyance, the old leader would turn on the three-year-old. Sometimes she turned with him. And sometimes the young leader on the left turned, too.

In these moments, faced with three sets of fierce teeth, the young wolf came to an abrupt halt, throwing himself backward onto his haunches with his front legs rigid, his mouth threatening, and his fur standing on end. This disruption at the front of the moving pack invariably created chaos behind him. The wolves following crashed into the young wolf and showed their irritation by delivering sharp bites to his hind legs and sides. He was creating problems for himself, since hunger and bad tempers naturally went hand in hand; but with the unlimited optimism of youth, he continued to repeat this same move again and again, even though it never brought him anything except embarrassment and failure.

If there had been food available, mating and fighting would have continued at full pace, and the pack structure would have fallen apart. But the pack's situation was dire. The wolves were gaunt from prolonged starvation. They moved slower than their normal pace. The weakest members—the very young and the very old—struggled behind at the back. The strongest wolves led at the front. Still, all of them looked more like skeletons than healthy, full-bodied wolves. Even so, except for those that were limping, the animals moved with ease and endless endurance. Their lean muscles seemed like sources of unlimited energy. Behind every steel-like muscle contraction lay another steel-like contraction, and another, and another, seemingly without end.

They covered many miles that day. They kept running through the night. When the next day arrived, they were still running. They moved across the surface of a world that was frozen and lifeless. Nothing else was moving. They were the only ones traveling through the enormous stillness. They were the only living things, and they searched for other living creatures so they could eat them and stay alive.

They crossed low ridges and traveled through a dozen small streams in the lower terrain before their search paid off. Then they discovered moose. The first one they encountered was a large bull. Here was meat and survival, and it wasn't protected by any mysterious fires or flying flaming projectiles. They recognized the broad hooves and flat antlers, and they threw their usual patience and caution aside. The battle was short but intense. The massive bull was attacked from all directions. He tore them open or cracked their skulls with skillfully aimed strikes from his powerful hooves. He crushed and broke them with his enormous antlers. He trampled them into the snow beneath him during the chaotic struggle. But his fate was sealed, and he collapsed with the she-wolf savagely ripping at his throat, while other teeth latched onto him everywhere, eating him alive, even before his final struggles ended or his last blow had been delivered.

There was plenty of food. The bull weighed more than eight hundred pounds—a full twenty pounds of meat for each of the forty or so wolves in the pack. But just as they could go without food for incredibly long periods, they could also eat enormous amounts, and before long only a few scattered bones were left of the magnificent living animal that had confronted the pack just a few hours earlier.

There was now plenty of time for rest and sleep. With their bellies full, the younger males started fighting and arguing with each other, and this behavior continued for several days until the pack eventually split apart. The period of starvation had ended. The wolves had reached territory rich with prey, and while they still hunted together as a group, they became more selective in their approach, targeting heavy cows or injured old bulls from the small moose herds they encountered.

There came a day, in this abundant land, when the wolf pack divided in two and headed in opposite directions. The she-wolf, with the young leader at her left side and the one-eyed elder at her right, guided their portion of the pack down toward the Mackenzie River and across into the eastern lake region. With each passing day, this remaining fragment of the pack grew smaller. In pairs, male and female, the wolves were abandoning the group. Sometimes a lone male was forced out by the fierce teeth of competing wolves. Eventually, only four wolves remained: the she-wolf, the young leader, the one-eyed wolf, and the determined three-year-old.

The she-wolf had developed a fierce and aggressive temperament by this point. All three of her male admirers carried the scars from her bites. However, they never fought back or tried to protect themselves from her attacks. They would expose their backs to her most vicious strikes, wagging their tails and taking careful steps as they tried to calm her fury. While they showed complete gentleness toward her, they displayed nothing but aggression toward each other. The three-year-old became overly bold in his attacks. He approached the one-eyed older wolf from his blind side and tore his ear to shreds. Although the gray-muzzled veteran could only see from one side, he used the wisdom gained from many years of experience against his younger and stronger opponent. His missing eye and battle-scarred snout told the story of what kind of experience he possessed. He had lived through too many fights to hesitate even for a second about his next move.

The fight started on equal terms, but it didn't finish that way. No one could have predicted how it would turn out, because the third wolf came to help the older one, and together—the old leader and the young leader—they turned on the ambitious three-year-old and began to tear him apart. He found himself trapped between the ruthless teeth of his former allies. Gone were the memories of hunting side by side, the prey they had brought down together, the hunger they had endured as one. Those days were behind them now. The matter of love had taken over—always a harsher and more brutal affair than the struggle for survival.

And meanwhile, the she-wolf, who had caused all of this, sat down comfortably on her hind legs and watched. She was even happy about it. This was her special day—and it didn't happen very often—when fur stood on end, and teeth clashed against teeth or slashed and shredded the soft flesh, all because the males were fighting over her.

And in matters of love, the three-year-old wolf, who had made this his first romantic venture, gave up his life. On both sides of his body stood his two competitors. They were staring at the female wolf, who sat grinning in the snow. But the older leader was clever, extremely clever, in romance just as he was in combat. The younger leader turned his head to tend to a wound on his shoulder. The bend of his neck was exposed toward his opponent. With his single eye, the elder spotted the chance. He lunged in low and struck with his teeth. It was a long, tearing gash, and deep too. His fangs, as they passed through, ruptured the wall of the major artery in the throat. Then he sprang back to safety.

The young leader growled fiercely, but his growl turned into a hacking cough halfway through. Bleeding and coughing, already wounded, he lunged at the older man and continued fighting as his life ebbed away, his legs growing weak beneath him, the daylight dimming in his eyes, his strikes and leaps becoming weaker and weaker.

And throughout this entire time, the female wolf remained seated on her hind legs, wearing what appeared to be a smile. The battle brought her a kind of undefined joy, because this represented the courtship rituals of the wilderness, the reproductive drama of the natural world that only seemed tragic to those who perished. For those who lived through it, this wasn't tragedy at all, but rather fulfillment and success.

When the young leader lay motionless in the snow, One Eye approached the she-wolf. He carried himself with a mixture of victory and wariness. He clearly expected to be rejected, and he was obviously surprised when her teeth didn't snap at him in fury. For the first time, she greeted him with a gentle attitude. She touched noses with him and even lowered herself to jump around and play with him in a very puppy-like way. And despite all his gray years and wise experience, he acted just as much like a puppy and even a bit more foolishly.

The defeated rivals and the bloody love story written in the snow had already faded from memory. They were forgotten, except for one brief moment when old One Eye paused to lick his wounds as they grew stiff. In that instant, his lips nearly curled into a snarl, and the fur on his neck and shoulders bristled without his control, while he crouched halfway down ready to leap, his claws gripping spasmodically into the snowy ground for better footing. But all of this was forgotten the very next moment, as he bounded after the she-wolf, who was playfully leading him on a chase through the forest.

After that they ran side by side, like good friends who had reached an understanding. The days went by, and they stayed together, hunting their food and killing and eating it together. After some time the female wolf began to grow restless. She seemed to be looking for something that she couldn't find. The hollow spaces under fallen trees seemed to draw her attention, and she spent a lot of time sniffing around among the larger snow-covered cracks in the rocks and in the caves beneath overhanging riverbanks. Old One Eye wasn't interested at all, but he followed her good-naturedly in her search, and when her explorations in certain places took unusually long, he would lie down and wait until she was ready to move on.

They didn't stay in one place, but traveled across the countryside until they reached the Mackenzie River again, moving slowly downstream and frequently leaving it to hunt for game along the smaller streams that flowed into it, though they always came back to the main river. Occasionally they came across other wolves, typically in pairs, but neither side showed any friendliness in their interactions—no joy at meeting, no wish to form a pack again. Multiple times they ran into lone wolves. These were always males, and they persistently tried to join One Eye and his mate. He didn't like this, and when she stood beside him, bristling and baring her teeth, these hopeful loners would retreat, turn around, and go back to wandering alone.

One moonlit night, as he ran through the silent forest, One Eye suddenly stopped. He lifted his muzzle, his tail grew rigid, and his nostrils flared as he caught a scent in the air. He also raised one paw, like a dog would do. He wasn't satisfied, and he kept sniffing the air, trying to understand the message it carried to him. One casual sniff had been enough for his mate, and she trotted ahead to comfort him. Although he followed her, he remained uncertain, and he couldn't help stopping occasionally to examine the warning more carefully.

She carefully crept out to the edge of a large clearing surrounded by trees. For a while she stood there by herself. Then One Eye appeared, moving slowly and cautiously with every sense alert and every hair bristling with deep suspicion, and came to stand beside her. They remained there together, watching, listening, and sniffing the air.

The sounds of dogs fighting and wrestling reached their ears, along with the harsh shouts of men, the sharper voices of women scolding, and occasionally the high-pitched, mournful cry of a child. Apart from the massive shapes of the hide shelters, they could see little except the dancing flames of the fire, interrupted by the movement of bodies passing in front of it, and the smoke drifting upward in the still air. But their noses picked up the countless scents of an Indian camp, telling a story that was mostly meaningless to One Eye, but whose every detail the she-wolf understood.

She felt an unusual excitement stirring within her, breathing in the scents with growing pleasure. However, old One Eye remained uncertain. He revealed his worry and began hesitantly moving away. She turned and gently touched his neck with her nose to comfort him, then looked back at the camp once more. A new longing appeared on her face, though it wasn't the longing that comes from hunger. She felt a powerful urge driving her to move closer, to get nearer to that fire, to fight with the dogs, and to dodge and weave around the clumsy footsteps of the men.

One Eye shifted restlessly beside her; her anxiety returned, and she felt once more the urgent need to find what she was looking for. She turned and trotted back into the forest, much to One Eye's relief, who moved slightly ahead until they were safely within the protection of the trees.

As they glided forward, silent as shadows in the moonlight, they discovered a trail. Both wolves lowered their noses to examine the footprints in the snow. These tracks were extremely fresh. One Eye moved ahead carefully, with his mate following close behind. The wide pads of their feet spread out against the snow, touching it like velvet. One Eye spotted a faint movement of white against the white landscape. His gliding pace had been misleadingly quick, but it was nothing compared to the speed at which he now raced. Ahead of him bounced the pale white shape he had spotted.

They raced down a narrow path bordered by young spruce trees on both sides. The end of the path was visible through the branches, opening into a clearing bathed in moonlight. Old One Eye was quickly catching up to the fleeing white figure. With each leap, he closed the distance. Now he was right behind it. One more jump and his teeth would sink into his prey. But that final leap never happened. High above him, shooting straight upward, the white shape soared—revealed now as a frantic snowshoe rabbit that jumped and bounced, performing an incredible dance in the air above him, never touching the ground again.

One Eye jumped back with a sudden snort of alarm, then dropped low to the snow and crouched there, growling menacingly at this frightening thing he couldn't comprehend. But the she-wolf calmly pushed past him. She paused for an instant, then leaped toward the bouncing rabbit. She also flew high into the air, but not as high as her prey, and her jaws snapped shut on nothing but air with a sharp metallic click. She attempted another jump, and then another.

Her partner had gradually eased out of his crouched position and was observing her. He now showed irritation at her repeated attempts that had failed, and decided to make a powerful leap upward himself. His teeth clamped down on the rabbit, and he pulled it back down to the ground with him. But at the same moment there was a worrying crackling sound next to him, and his startled eyes witnessed a young spruce tree bending down toward him as if to strike. His jaws released their hold, and he jumped backward to avoid this unusual threat, his lips pulled back to reveal his fangs, his throat growling, every strand of fur standing on end with anger and fear. And in that instant the young tree straightened its thin trunk upright and the rabbit flew dancing through the air once more.

The she-wolf was furious. She bit down hard with her fangs into her mate's shoulder as a rebuke, and he, startled and not understanding what had triggered this sudden attack, lashed back savagely and with even greater panic, tearing open the side of the she-wolf's snout. His hostile response to her scolding caught her completely off guard, and she lunged at him with growling rage. Then he realized his error and attempted to calm her down. But she continued to discipline him thoroughly, until he abandoned all efforts to appease her and spun around in circles, turning his head away from her while his shoulders bore the brunt of her punishing bites.

In the meantime the rabbit danced above them in the air. The she-wolf sat down in the snow, and old One Eye, now more afraid of his mate than of the mysterious sapling, jumped for the rabbit again. As he fell back with it between his teeth, he kept watching the sapling. Just like before, it followed him back to the ground. He crouched down under the coming blow, his fur standing on

47

end, but his teeth still gripping the rabbit tightly. But the blow never came. The sapling stayed bent above him. When he moved it moved, and he snarled at it through his clenched jaws; when he stayed still, it stayed still, and he decided it was safer to keep staying still. Yet the warm blood of the rabbit tasted good in his mouth.

His mate rescued him from the difficult situation he was in. She took the rabbit from him, and while the young tree swayed and rocked dangerously overhead, she calmly chewed off the rabbit's head. Immediately the sapling sprang upright, and after that caused no further problems, staying in the proper vertical position that nature had meant for it to grow. Then, working together, the she-wolf and One Eye ate the prey that the strange sapling had captured for them.

There were other trails and pathways where rabbits hung suspended in the air, and the wolf pair explored every one of them, with the female wolf taking the lead while old One Eye followed behind, watching carefully and learning how to steal from traps— knowledge that would serve him well in the future.

Chapter II: The Lair

For two days, the she-wolf and One Eye lingered around the Indian camp. He felt anxious and uneasy, yet the camp attracted his mate and she was reluctant to leave. But when, one morning, the air was shattered by the crack of a rifle nearby, and a bullet struck a tree trunk just inches from One Eye's head, they no longer hesitated, but departed in a long, steady run that quickly put many miles between them and the threat.

They didn't travel far—just a couple of days' journey. The she-wolf's need to find what she was searching for had become urgent. She was getting very heavy and could only run slowly. Once, while chasing a rabbit that she normally would have caught easily, she gave up and lay down to rest. One Eye came over to her, but when he gently touched her neck with his muzzle, she snapped at him so quickly and fiercely that he tumbled backward and looked foolish trying to escape her teeth. Her temper was shorter than ever, but he had become more patient and caring than before.

And then she discovered what she had been looking for. It was located a few miles upstream along a small waterway that during summer flowed into the Mackenzie River, but was now completely frozen solid all the way down to its rocky bottom—a lifeless stretch of solid white ice extending from beginning to end. The female wolf was moving forward with tired steps, her partner far ahead of her, when she came across the jutting, tall clay embankment. She changed direction and padded over to examine it. The damage from spring storms and melting snow had eroded the base of the bank, and in one spot had carved out a small cave from what had once been a narrow crack.

She stopped at the cave entrance and examined the wall thoroughly. Then she ran along the base of the wall on both sides, following it to where its steep mass blended into the gentler contours of the surrounding landscape. Coming back to the cave, she squeezed through its narrow opening. For about three feet, she had to crouch down, but then the walls expanded and the ceiling rose higher, creating a small circular chamber almost six feet across. The roof just barely cleared the top of her head. The space was dry and comfortable. She examined it with meticulous attention while One Eye, who had come back, stood at the entrance watching her patiently. She lowered her head with her nose pointing toward the ground, aiming at a spot near her tightly gathered paws, and she walked in circles around this spot several times. Then, with a weary sigh that sounded almost like a grunt, she curled up her body, relaxed her legs, and lay down with her head facing the entrance. One Eye watched her with alert, curious ears and seemed to smile at her, and beyond him, silhouetted against the bright light, she could see his tail swishing in a friendly manner. Her own ears moved in a settling motion, folding their pointed tips backward and down against her head for a moment, while her mouth opened and her tongue hung out peacefully, showing that she felt pleased and content.

One Eye was hungry. Although he lay down at the entrance and slept, his sleep was restless. He kept waking up and tilting his ears toward the bright world outside, where the April sun blazed across the snow. When he drifted off, the faint whispers of hidden streams of running water would reach his ears, and he would wake up and listen carefully. The sun had returned, and all the awakening northern world was calling to him. Life was stirring. The feeling of spring was in the air, the feeling of growing life beneath the snow, of sap rising in the trees, of buds breaking free from the grip of frost.

He glanced nervously at his partner, but she displayed no interest in rising. He peered outside, where half a dozen snow-birds darted through his view. He began to stand, then glanced back at his mate once more, and settled back down to rest. A sharp, tiny sound reached his ears. Once, then twice, he drowsily rubbed his nose with his paw. Then he awakened. There, hovering in the air right at the tip of his nose, was a solitary mosquito. It was a fully developed mosquito, one that had remained frozen inside a dried log throughout the winter and had just been warmed back to life by the sun. He could no longer resist the world's calling. Moreover, he was hungry.

He crawled over to his companion and attempted to convince her to stand up. However, she simply growled at him, so he ventured out by himself into the brilliant sunlight to discover the snow's surface was soft beneath his feet and walking was challenging. He traveled up the frozen streambed, where the snow, sheltered by the trees, remained hard and crystal-like. He was away for eight hours, and he returned through the darkness more famished than when he had departed. He had located prey, but he had failed to capture it. He had fallen through the melting snow crust and struggled through it, while the snowshoe rabbits had glided across the surface as effortlessly as always.

He stopped at the cave entrance, suddenly filled with suspicion. Soft, unusual sounds drifted from inside. These weren't sounds his mate would make, yet something about them seemed vaguely familiar. He crept carefully into the cave on his belly and was greeted by a threatening growl from the female wolf. This didn't disturb him, though he respected the warning by staying back; however, he remained curious about the other sounds—quiet, muted whimpering and wet, slobbering noises.

His mate snapped at him irritably, driving him away, so he curled up and fell asleep in the entrance. When morning arrived and a faint light filled the den, he once again searched for the source of those distantly familiar sounds. There was something different in his mate's warning growl. It carried a jealous tone, and he was extremely cautious to maintain a respectful distance. Even so, he managed to see, nestled between her legs against the length of her body, five odd little bundles of life, extremely weak, completely helpless, making soft whimpering sounds, with eyes that remained closed to the light. He was astonished. This wasn't the first time in his long and prosperous life that this event had occurred. It had taken place many times before, yet each time it struck him as fresh and surprising as it had ever been.

His mate watched him with worry. Every so often she let out a quiet growl, and sometimes, when she felt he was getting too close, the growl would rise in her throat to become a sharp snarl. She had no personal memory of this kind of thing happening before; but deep in her instincts, which carried the experiences of all wolf mothers before her, there remained a memory of fathers who had devoured their newborn and defenseless offspring. This showed itself as a powerful fear inside her, which made her keep

51

One Eye from getting a closer look at the cubs he had fathered.

But there was no danger. Old One Eye was feeling the pull of an urge, which was itself an instinct that had been passed down to him from all the wolf fathers before him. He didn't question it or wonder about it. It existed in the very core of his being, and it was the most natural thing in the world for him to follow it by turning away from his newborn family and trotting off along the hunting trail that sustained his life.

Five or six miles away from the den, the creek split into two branches that headed off into the mountains at right angles to each other. At this point, following the left branch upstream, he discovered a fresh set of tracks. He sniffed at them and realized they were so recent that he quickly dropped into a crouch and peered in the direction where they vanished. After that, he deliberately turned around and chose the right branch instead. The footprints were much bigger than those his own feet would leave, and he understood that following such a trail would yield very little food for him.

Half a mile up the right fork, his sharp ears picked up the sound of gnawing teeth. He tracked his prey and discovered it was a porcupine, standing upright against a tree and testing its teeth on the bark. One Eye moved closer with caution but little hope. He recognized this type of animal, though he had never encountered one this far north before; and never in his entire life had a porcupine provided him with a meal. However, he had learned long ago that such things as Chance, or Opportunity, existed, and he kept moving closer. There was no way to predict what might occur, because with living creatures things always seemed to unfold in unexpected ways.

The porcupine curled itself into a tight ball, sending long, razor-sharp quills outward in every direction that made any attack impossible. During his younger days, One Eye had once gotten too close to a similar, seemingly motionless bundle of spines, and the tail had suddenly whipped out and struck him in the face. He had carried one quill away embedded in his snout, where it remained for weeks as a burning torment, until it eventually worked its way out. So he settled down into a comfortable crouching stance, keeping his nose a full foot away and well clear of the tail's reach. He waited in this position, remaining completely still. There was no way to predict what might occur. Something could change. The porcupine might uncurl itself. There could be a chance for a quick and devastating strike of his paw into the soft, exposed belly.

But after thirty minutes, he got up, snarled angrily at the still ball, and moved on. He had waited too many times before for porcupines to uncurl themselves, only to be disappointed, and he wasn't going to waste any more time. He kept going up the right fork. The day passed, and his hunt yielded nothing.

The powerful urge of his newly awakened paternal instinct drove him forward. He had to find food. During the afternoon, he stumbled across a ptarmigan. He emerged from a dense cluster of bushes and suddenly found himself staring directly at the sluggish bird. The creature was perched on a fallen log, less than a foot from the tip of his nose. Both animals spotted each other simultaneously. The bird attempted a panicked takeoff, but he swatted it with his paw and knocked it crashing to the ground, then leaped on top of it and seized it between his jaws as it scrambled across the snow desperately trying to become airborne once more. As his teeth crushed through the soft meat and delicate bones, he instinctively began to feed. Then he recalled his purpose, and reversing direction along his previous path, he headed back home with the ptarmigan gripped firmly in his mouth.

A mile beyond where the streams joined together, moving silently with his usual soft steps, like a gliding shadow that carefully examined each new section of the path ahead, he discovered more recent prints of the large tracks he had found earlier that morning.

Since the trail was heading in his direction, he followed it, ready to encounter whoever had made these tracks at every bend in the stream.

He moved his head around a rocky corner where the stream took an unusually wide turn, and his sharp eyes spotted something that made him quickly duck down. It was the creature that had made the tracks—a large female lynx. She was crouched just as he had crouched earlier that day, facing the tightly curled ball of quills in front of her. If he had moved like a gliding shadow before, he now became the ghost of such a shadow as he crept in a wide circle, positioning himself downwind of the silent, motionless pair.

He lay down in the snow, placing the ptarmigan next to him, and peered through the needles of a low-growing spruce to watch the drama of life unfolding before him—the waiting lynx and the waiting porcupine, each focused on survival; and, such was the strange nature of this game, survival for one meant devouring the other, while survival for the other meant avoiding being devoured. Meanwhile, old One Eye, the wolf crouched in his hiding place, also played his role in this game, waiting for some unexpected twist of fate that might lead him to the meat he needed for his own survival.

Half an hour went by, then a full hour, and still nothing occurred. The porcupine could have been a rock for how little it stirred; the lynx appeared frozen like marble; and old One Eye seemed lifeless. Despite this, all three creatures were wound tight with an intensity of existence that bordered on agony, and rarely would they experience being more vibrantly alive than they were in that moment of apparent stillness.

One Eye shifted slightly and looked out with growing intensity. Something was taking place. The porcupine had finally concluded that its enemy had departed. Gradually, carefully, it was unwinding its sphere of impenetrable armor. No shiver of expectation disturbed it. Slowly, deliberately, the spiky ball extended and stretched out. One Eye, observing, experienced a sudden wetness in his mouth and a flow of saliva, automatic, stirred by the living flesh that was displaying itself like a feast before him.

The porcupine hadn't completely unrolled when it spotted its enemy. At that moment, the lynx attacked. The strike came like a lightning flash. Its paw, with stiff claws curved like talons, shot beneath the soft belly and pulled back with a quick tearing motion. If the porcupine had been fully unrolled, or if it hadn't noticed its enemy just a split second before the strike landed, the paw would have gotten away without injury; but a sideways whip of the tail drove sharp quills into it as it pulled back.

Everything had happened at once—the blow, the counter-blow, the squeal of agony from the porcupine, the big cat's squall of sudden hurt and astonishment. One Eye half arose in his excitement, his ears up, his tail straight out and quivering behind him. The lynx's bad temper got the best of her. She sprang savagely at the thing that had hurt her. But the porcupine, squealing and grunting, with disrupted anatomy trying feebly to roll up into its ball-protection, flicked out its tail again, and again the big cat squalled with hurt and astonishment. Then she fell to backing away and sneezing, her nose bristling with quills like a monstrous pin-cushion. She brushed her nose with her paws, trying to dislodge the fiery darts, thrust it into the snow, and rubbed it against twigs and branches, and all the time leaping about, ahead, sidewise, up and down, in a frenzy of pain and fright.

She kept sneezing nonstop, and her short stub of a tail was doing everything it could to thrash around by making quick, sharp jerks. She stopped her wild behavior and settled down for a full minute. One Eye kept watching. Even he couldn't help but jump and feel his hair bristle along his back when she suddenly launched herself straight up into the air without any warning, letting out a long and absolutely terrifying shriek at the same time. Then she bounded away up the trail, shrieking with each leap she took.

One Eye didn't dare to come out until the sound of her commotion had completely disappeared into the distance. He moved with extreme caution, as if the entire snowy ground was covered with sharp porcupine quills standing upright, ready to stab into the tender pads of his paws. The porcupine responded to his approach with angry shrieking and the grinding of its long teeth. It had succeeded in curling itself into a ball once more, but this wasn't the same tight, solid ball as before; its muscles had been torn too severely for that. The creature had been slashed nearly in two and was still losing a great deal of blood.

One Eye gathered mouthfuls of the blood-stained snow, chewing and tasting before swallowing it down. This acted like seasoning, and his appetite grew tremendously; however, he had lived too long to abandon his wariness. He waited patiently. He settled down and remained still, while the porcupine ground its teeth and made grunting sounds, sobs, and occasional sharp little cries. After some time, One Eye observed that the quills were beginning to droop and that intense trembling had begun. The shaking stopped abruptly. There was one last defiant grinding of the long teeth. Then all the quills sagged completely, and the body went limp and became motionless.

With a cautious, hesitant paw, One Eye extended the porcupine to its complete length and flipped it onto its back. Nothing occurred. It was certainly dead. He examined it carefully for a moment, then secured a cautious grip with his teeth and began moving down the stream, partially carrying, partially dragging the porcupine, with his head turned sideways to avoid stepping on the spiky body. He remembered something, dropped his load, and trotted back to where he had left the ptarmigan. He didn't hesitate for a moment. He understood exactly what needed to be done, and he accomplished this by quickly eating the ptarmigan. Then he went back and picked up his burden.

When he pulled the day's catch into the cave, the female wolf examined it, turned her snout toward him, and gently licked his neck. However, the very next moment she was driving him away from the pups with a growl that was softer than normal and seemed more like an apology than a threat. Her natural fear of the father of her offspring was beginning to fade. He was acting like a proper wolf father should, showing no unnatural urge to consume the young lives she had brought into existence.

Chapter III: The Grey Cub

He was unlike his brothers and sisters. Their fur already showed the reddish tint they had inherited from their mother, the she-wolf, while he alone resembled his father in this way. He was the single little gray cub in the litter. He had inherited the pure wolf bloodline—indeed, he had taken after old One Eye himself in appearance, with only one difference: he had both eyes while his father had just one.

The grey cub had only recently opened his eyes, but he could already see with clear, steady vision. Even before his eyes had opened, he had experienced the world through feeling, tasting, and smelling. He was thoroughly familiar with his two brothers and two sisters. He had started playing with them in a weak, clumsy manner, and had even begun fighting with them, his small throat producing a strange scratching sound that would later become a growl as he worked himself into a rage. Long before he could see, he had learned through touch, taste, and smell to recognize his mother—a source of warmth, milk, and gentle care. She had a soft, loving tongue that comforted him when she licked his tender little body, making him want to curl up close to her and drift off to sleep.

Most of his first month had been spent sleeping, but now he could see clearly and stayed awake for longer stretches, gradually becoming familiar with his surroundings. His world was dark and dreary, though he didn't realize this since he had never known anything different. The lighting was always dim, but his eyes had never needed to adapt to any other kind of illumination. His world was incredibly small, bounded by the walls of the den, yet since he had no awareness of the vast world beyond, the tight confines of his life never felt restrictive to him.

But he had discovered early on that one wall of his world was different from all the others. This was the cave's entrance and where the light came from. He had realized it was unlike the other walls long before he had developed his own thoughts or conscious desires. It had drawn him irresistibly even before his eyes had opened to see it. The light from it had struck his closed eyelids, and his eyes and optic nerves had responded with tiny, spark-like flashes that were warm in color and mysteriously pleasant. The life force within his body, within every fiber of his being—the life that formed the very essence of his physical form and existed separately from his individual consciousness—had longed for this light and pushed his body toward it in the same manner that a plant's intricate chemistry drives it toward the sun.

From the very beginning, before he became aware of himself, he had always crawled toward the cave's entrance. His brothers and sisters did exactly the same thing. During that early time, none of them ever crawled toward the dark corners at the back of the cave. The light pulled them forward like plants reaching for the sun; their very life force required light to survive, and their small bodies moved instinctively and automatically toward it, much like vine shoots growing toward brightness. As time passed and each of them developed their own personality and became aware of their own urges and wants, the pull of the light grew even stronger. They constantly crawled and scrambled toward it, only to be pushed back by their mother again and again.

This is how the grey cub discovered other qualities of his mother beyond her gentle, comforting tongue. As he persistently crawled toward the light, he found that she had a nose that could deliver sharp nudges as punishment, and later, a paw that could pin him down and tumble him around with quick, deliberate movements. Through this, he learned what pain was; and beyond that, he learned how to avoid pain in two ways: first, by not taking risks that might lead to it; and second, when he had already taken such risks, by dodging and retreating. These were deliberate actions that came from his first basic understanding of how the world worked. Before this learning, he had pulled back from pain instinctively, just as he had crawled toward light instinctively. After this learning, he pulled back from pain because he understood what pain was.

He was a fierce little cub. His brothers and sisters were equally fierce. This was only natural. He was a meat-eating animal. He descended from a lineage of killers and flesh-eaters. His father and mother survived entirely on meat. The milk he had nursed during his earliest moments of life was milk created directly from meat, and now, at one month old, when his eyes had only been open for a week, he was starting to eat meat himself—meat that had been partially digested by the she-wolf and brought back up for the five growing cubs who were already demanding too much from her milk.

But he was also the most aggressive of the group. He could produce a louder, harsher growl than any of his siblings. His small fits of anger were far more intense than theirs. He was the first to master the technique of knocking over a brother or sister with a clever swipe of his paw. And he was the first to grab another cub by the ear and pull and tug while growling through clenched teeth. And without question, he was the one who gave their mother the greatest difficulty in keeping her young away from the cave entrance.

The grey cub's fascination with the light grew stronger each day. He constantly set off on yard-long journeys toward the cave's entrance, only to be repeatedly driven back. But he didn't understand it was an entrance. He knew nothing about entrances—pathways that lead from one place to another. He was unaware of any other place, let alone how to reach it. To him, the cave's entrance appeared as a wall—a wall made of light. Just as the sun meant everything to those living outside, this wall served as the sun of his entire world. It drew him in the way a candle draws a moth. He was always trying to reach it. The life force rapidly growing inside him constantly pushed him toward this wall of light. The life within him understood this was the only way out, the path he was meant to follow. Yet he himself knew nothing about this. He had no idea that an outside world even existed.

There was something peculiar about this barrier of light. His father—he had already learned to recognize his father as the other inhabitant of their world, a being similar to his mother who rested close to the light and brought food—had a habit of walking straight into the bright distant barrier and vanishing. The young gray cub couldn't comprehend this phenomenon. Although his mother never allowed him to go near that particular barrier, he had explored the other barriers and met with solid resistance against his delicate nose. This caused pain. After experiencing several such encounters, he avoided the barriers entirely. Without contemplating it, he came to accept this vanishing into the barrier as one of his father's unique traits, just as milk and partially digested meat were unique traits of his mother.

The grey cub wasn't one for deep thinking—at least not the type of thinking that humans do. His mind operated in unclear, instinctive ways. Still, his conclusions were just as precise and clear as those reached by people. He had his own way of accepting reality without questioning why things were the way they were.

This was really a form of categorizing the world around him. He never worried about why something occurred. Understanding how it happened was enough for him. So when he had knocked his nose against the back wall several times, he came to accept that he couldn't pass through solid barriers. In the same manner, he accepted that his father had the ability to vanish through walls. Yet he felt no urge whatsoever to understand why he and his father were different in this regard. Logical reasoning and understanding physical laws weren't part of how his mind worked.

Like most wild animals, he faced starvation early in life. A time came when not only did the food disappear, but his mother's milk stopped flowing as well. Initially, the young cubs whined and cried, though they mostly slept. Before long, they had fallen into a hunger-induced stupor. The fighting and quarreling stopped, along with the small bursts of anger and attempts to growl; meanwhile, their explorations toward the distant white wall came to a complete halt. The cubs slept while the life force within them grew weaker and began to fade away.

One Eye was desperate. He roamed far and wide, sleeping very little in the den that had become gloomy and wretched. The she-wolf also left her young and ventured out to hunt for food. During the first days following the birth of the cubs, One Eye had traveled back to the Indian camp multiple times to steal from the rabbit traps; however, as the snow melted and the streams began flowing, the Indian camp had relocated, cutting off that food source for him.

When the grey cub regained consciousness and once again showed interest in the distant white wall, he discovered that his world's population had diminished. Only one sister remained with him. The others had disappeared. As his strength returned, he found himself forced to play by himself, since his sister no longer raised her head or moved around. His small body filled out from the meat he was now eating, but the nourishment had arrived too late for her. She slept without interruption, a small skeleton wrapped in skin where the spark of life grew dimmer and dimmer until it finally extinguished.

Then there came a time when the grey cub no longer saw his father appearing and disappearing in the wall nor lying down asleep in the entrance. This had happened at the end of a second and less severe famine. The she-wolf knew why One Eye never came back, but there was no way by which she could tell what she had seen to the grey cub. Hunting herself for meat, up the left fork of the stream where lived the lynx, she had followed a day-old trail of One Eye. And she had found him, or what remained of him, at the end of the trail. There were many signs of the battle that had been fought, and of the lynx's withdrawal to her lair after having won the victory. Before she went away, the she-wolf had found this lair, but the signs told her that the lynx was inside, and she had not dared to venture in.

After that, the she-wolf avoided the left fork when hunting. She was aware that the lynx's den contained a litter of young, and she understood the lynx to be a fierce, ill-tempered animal and a formidable fighter. It was one thing for six wolves to chase a lynx, hissing and with fur standing on end, up into a tree; but it was entirely different for a solitary wolf to face a lynx—particularly when the lynx was known to have a litter of hungry young ones to protect.

But the wilderness remains the wilderness, and motherhood is motherhood, always fiercely protective whether in the wild or beyond it; and the time would come when the she-wolf, for the sake of her grey cub, would risk taking the left fork, approaching the den in the rocks, and facing the lynx's fury.

Chapter IV: The Wall Of The World

By the time his mother started leaving the cave to hunt, the young cub had thoroughly learned the rule that prevented him from going near the entrance. This rule hadn't just been taught to him once—his mother's nose and paw had enforced it repeatedly and firmly. Beyond this physical teaching, something deeper was growing within him: the instinct of fear. Throughout his short life in the cave, he had never come across anything that should have frightened him. Still, fear lived inside him. This emotion had traveled down to him from distant ancestors across countless generations. It was an inheritance he had received directly from One Eye and the she-wolf, but they too had inherited it from all the wolf generations that came before them. Fear—that gift from the wilderness that no animal can avoid or trade away.

The grey cub understood fear, even though he didn't know what fear was actually made of. He probably accepted it as just another limitation of life. After all, he had already discovered that such limitations existed. He had experienced hunger before, and when he couldn't satisfy that hunger, he had felt restricted. The solid barrier of the cave wall, the sharp poke from his mother's nose, the powerful blow of her paw, and the unsatisfied hunger during several periods of starvation had taught him that the world wasn't completely free, that life came with boundaries and restrictions. These boundaries and restrictions were laws. Following them meant avoiding pain and finding happiness.

He didn't think through the problem in this logical way. He simply sorted things into two categories: what caused him pain and what didn't. After organizing them this way, he stayed away from the painful things—the limitations and constraints—so he could enjoy life's pleasures and rewards.

Because of this, following the rule his mother had established and obeying the law of that mysterious and unnamed force called fear, he stayed away from the cave entrance. To him, it remained a bright wall of light. When his mother wasn't there, he spent most of his time sleeping, and during the moments when he was awake, he stayed completely still, holding back the soft whining sounds that rose in his throat and wanted to break free as noise.

Once, while lying awake, he heard an unusual sound coming from the white wall. He had no idea it was a wolverine standing outside, trembling with its own boldness and carefully trying to smell what was inside the cave. The cub only knew that this scent was unfamiliar, something he couldn't identify, which made it unknown and frightening—because the unknown was one of the main things that created fear.

The fur on the grey cub's back stood on end, though it rose without a sound. How could he possibly know that this sniffing creature was something to fear? This reaction didn't come from any learned experience, yet it showed the terror he felt inside— terror he couldn't explain or understand in his short life. But along with fear came another natural response: the need to hide. The cub was overwhelmed with panic, yet he remained completely still and silent, frozen solid, appearing lifeless to anyone watching. When his mother returned home, she growled upon catching the wolverine's scent, then rushed into the cave and licked and nudged him with unusually intense affection. The cub sensed that he had somehow avoided serious danger.

But other forces were working inside the cub, and the most powerful of these was growth. Instinct and natural law required him to obey. However, growth demanded rebellion. His mother and fear drove him to stay away from the white wall. Growth represents life, and life is forever meant to reach toward the light. Therefore, nothing could hold back the surge of life that was building within him—growing stronger with every bite of meat he ate, with every breath he took. Finally, one day, fear and obedience were overwhelmed by the force of life, and the cub stretched and crawled toward the entrance.

Unlike any other wall he had encountered before, this one seemed to pull back as he moved closer. No solid surface struck the delicate little nose he cautiously extended in front of him. The material of the wall felt as penetrable and flexible as light itself. And since condition appeared to take the form of shape in his perception, he stepped into what had seemed like a wall to him and immersed himself in the substance that made it up.

It was completely confusing. He was moving through what should have been solid matter. And the light kept getting brighter and brighter. Fear told him to turn around and go back, but his need to grow pushed him forward. All at once he reached the opening of the cave. The wall that he had believed surrounded him suddenly shot away from him to an incredible distance. The light had become so bright it hurt. It blinded him. At the same time, this sudden and enormous expansion of space made him feel dizzy. Without thinking about it, his eyes began adapting to the brightness, adjusting their focus to handle objects that were now much farther away. At first, the wall had jumped so far back that he couldn't see it anymore. Now he could see it again, but it seemed remarkably far away. Its appearance had also transformed. What he now saw was a multicolored wall made up of the trees that lined the stream, the mountain rising high above those trees, and the sky that stretched even higher than the mountain.

A tremendous fear overwhelmed him. This represented yet another encounter with the terrifying unknown. He crouched down at the edge of the cave and stared out at the world before him. Terror gripped him completely. Since this world was unfamiliar, it felt threatening to him. As a result, the fur along his spine bristled upright and his lips curled feebly as he tried to produce a fierce and menacing growl. From his small size and terror, he defied and threatened the entire vast world.

Nothing occurred. He kept staring, and his fascination made him forget to growl. He also forgot to feel frightened. At that moment, fear had been overcome by development, while development had taken on the appearance of curiosity. He started to observe nearby things—an exposed section of the creek that sparkled in the sunlight, the damaged pine tree that stood at the bottom of the hill, and the hill itself, which extended right up to where he was and stopped two feet below the edge of the cave where he was crouching.

The grey cub had spent his entire life on flat ground. He had never felt the pain of falling. He didn't understand what falling meant. So he confidently stepped out into empty air. His back legs were still on the edge of the cave, causing him to tumble forward headfirst. The ground hit his nose hard, making him cry out. Then he started rolling down the hill, tumbling over and over. He was overwhelmed with terror. The unknown had finally caught him. It had grabbed him violently and was about to cause him terrible harm. His courage was now overcome by fear, and he yelped like any scared puppy.

The unknown force carried him toward some terrible harm he couldn't imagine, and he yelped and cried out without stopping. This was completely different from crouching in frozen fear while the unknown presence lurked nearby. Now the unknown had seized him firmly. Staying quiet wouldn't help him now. Moreover, it wasn't just fear that overwhelmed him, but pure terror.

But the slope became less steep, and grass covered its bottom. Here the cub slowed down. When he finally stopped, he let out one final agonized cry followed by a long, whimpering wail. Then, as naturally as if he had groomed himself a thousand times before in his life, he began licking away the dry clay that covered his fur.

After that, he sat up and looked around, like the first person from Earth who had landed on Mars. The cub had broken through the barrier of his world, the unknown had released its grip on him, and here he was, completely unharmed. But the first person on Mars would have felt less out of place than he did. Without any previous knowledge, without any warning that such a place existed, he found himself an explorer in a completely new world.

Now that the terrifying unknown had released its grip on him, he forgot that the unknown held any fears. He was only aware of curiosity about everything around him. He examined the grass below him, the moss-berry plant just ahead, and the lifeless trunk of the lightning-struck pine that stood at the edge of a clearing among the trees. A squirrel, scampering around the base of the trunk, suddenly encountered him and startled him greatly. He crouched down and growled. But the squirrel was equally frightened. It scrambled up the tree, and from a safe position chattered back angrily.

This boosted the young wolf's bravery, and although the woodpecker he came across next startled him, he continued boldly along his path. His confidence had grown so much that when a gray jay boldly jumped toward him, he swatted at it with a playful paw. What he got in return was a painful jab on the tip of his nose that made him crouch low and yelp. The sound he produced was too much for the gray jay, who flew away to safety.

The young wolf was beginning to understand the world around him. His foggy little brain had already started sorting things without him realizing it. Some things were alive, and others weren't. He also knew he needed to be careful around the living creatures. The non-living objects always stayed put, but the living ones moved around, and you never knew what they might do next. With living things, you had to expect the unexpected, and he needed to stay ready for anything.

He moved very awkwardly. He bumped into branches and other obstacles. A twig that seemed far away would suddenly strike him in the face or scrape against his side. The ground was uneven. Sometimes he took too big a step and banged his nose. Just as often he didn't step far enough and hurt his feet. Then there were the small rocks and stones that shifted beneath him when he stepped on them; and from this he learned that non-living things weren't all as firmly fixed in place as his cave was—he also discovered that small non-living objects were more likely than large ones to fall over or roll away. But each accident taught him something. The more he walked, the better his walking became. He was adapting. He was learning to control his muscle movements, to understand what his body could and couldn't do, to judge distances between objects, and between objects and himself.

He had beginner's luck. Born to hunt for food (though he didn't realize it), he stumbled upon prey right outside his own cave entrance on his first venture into the world. It was pure chance that he discovered the cleverly concealed ptarmigan nest. He tumbled right into it. He had tried to walk across the trunk of a fallen pine tree. The decaying bark crumbled beneath his feet, and with a desperate cry he tumbled down the curved slope, crashed through the leaves and stems of a small bush, and at the center of the bush, on the ground, landed right in the middle of seven ptarmigan chicks.

They made sounds, and initially he was scared of them. Then he realized they were very small, and he grew more confident. They moved around. He put his paw on one, and it moved even faster. This brought him pleasure. He sniffed it. He picked it up with his mouth. It squirmed and tickled his tongue. At the same time he became aware of feeling hungry. His jaws snapped shut. There was a crushing of delicate bones, and warm blood flowed in his mouth. It tasted good. This was meat, the same kind his mother gave him, except it was alive between his teeth and therefore better. So he ate the ptarmigan. He didn't stop until he had eaten the entire brood. Then he licked his lips in exactly the same way his mother did, and started to crawl out of the bush.

He ran into a feathered tornado. The rushing motion and beating of furious wings left him bewildered and unable to see. He tucked his head between his paws and cried out. The strikes became more intense. The mother ptarmigan was absolutely enraged. At that point, he grew angry too. He stood up, growling, lashing out with his paws. He bit down on one of the wings with his small teeth and pulled and yanked with determination. The ptarmigan fought back against him, raining down blows with her free wing. This was his first fight. He felt thrilled. He completely forgot about the mysterious unknown. Nothing scared him anymore. He was battling, clawing at a living creature that was attacking him. On top of that, this living creature was food. The desire to kill had taken hold of him. He had just killed small living things. Now he would kill a large living thing. He was too occupied and joyful to realize his own happiness. He was experiencing excitement and triumph in ways that were new to him and more intense than anything he had ever felt before.

He gripped the wing tightly and snarled through his clenched teeth. The ptarmigan pulled him out from the bush. When she wheeled around and attempted to drag him back into the bush's protection, he yanked her away from it and out into the clearing. Throughout this struggle she kept crying out and beating him with her free wing, while feathers scattered like falling snow. The intensity of his excitement was enormous. All the fighting instincts of his ancestry had awakened in him and were coursing through his veins. This was truly living, though he had no awareness of it. He was discovering his purpose in the world; he was fulfilling what he was born to do—hunting prey and fighting to kill it. He was proving his right to exist, and life can accomplish nothing greater; for life reaches its peak when it performs completely that which it was designed to do.

After some time, the ptarmigan stopped struggling. He continued to grip her wing, and they both lay on the ground staring at each other. He attempted to growl in a threatening, fierce manner. She pecked at his nose, which was already tender from earlier encounters. He flinched but maintained his hold. She pecked him repeatedly. His flinching turned to whimpering. He tried to pull back from her, unaware that his grip on her wing was dragging her along with him. A barrage of pecks struck his battered nose. The fighting spirit drained out of him, and he released his prey, turned around, and ran across the open ground in a humiliating retreat.

He settled down to rest on the far side of the clearing, close to where the bushes began, his tongue hanging out as his chest rose and fell rapidly with exhaustion, his nose still aching and making him whine softly. But while he rested there, he was suddenly overwhelmed by a sense that something dreadful was about to happen. The unknown, with all its frightening possibilities, crashed over him like a wave, and he instinctively pulled back deeper into the protection of the bush. As he moved, a gust of wind brushed against him, and a massive, winged creature glided past in threatening silence. A hawk, plunging down from the bright sky above, had come within inches of striking him.

While he lay hidden in the bush, recovering from his terror and looking out with fearful eyes, the mother ptarmigan on the far side of the clearing fluttered away from her destroyed nest. Her grief over what she had lost made her oblivious to the winged predator diving from above. But the cub witnessed everything, and it served as both a warning and a lesson—the hawk's rapid plunge from the sky, the brief moment its body skimmed just above the earth, the deadly strike of its claws into the ptarmigan's flesh, the ptarmigan's cry of pain and terror, and the hawk's swift ascent back into the blue sky, carrying its prey away.

It took a long time before the young wolf emerged from his hiding place. He had gained valuable knowledge. Living creatures served as food. They tasted good when eaten. However, living creatures that were big enough could inflict pain. It made more sense to consume small living creatures like young ptarmigan, and to avoid large living creatures like adult ptarmigan hens. Still, he experienced a small surge of determination, a hidden urge to engage in another fight with that ptarmigan hen—except the hawk had taken her away. Perhaps there were other ptarmigan hens around. He decided he would venture out and find them.

He walked down a sloping bank toward the stream. Water was completely foreign to him—he had never encountered it before. The surface appeared solid and reliable, with no visible bumps or dips. Confidently, he stepped onto what he thought was firm ground and immediately plunged downward, crying out in terror as the unfamiliar element engulfed him. The coldness shocked his system, making him gasp and breathe rapidly. Instead of the air that had always filled his lungs when he breathed, water rushed in. The choking sensation felt like dying itself. For him, this represented death. Though he had no understanding of what death actually meant, he carried within him the same survival instinct that all wild creatures possess. Death appeared to him as the ultimate suffering. It embodied everything mysterious and threatening about the unknown world—the final, unimaginable disaster that could befall him, something he couldn't comprehend but instinctively dreaded with every fiber of his being.

He surfaced, and the fresh air flooded into his open mouth. He didn't sink back down. As if it were something he'd always done, he kicked out with all his limbs and started swimming. The closest bank was just a yard away, but he had emerged facing away from it, and the first thing he saw was the far bank, which he immediately began swimming toward. The stream was narrow, but at this pool it spread out to about twenty feet across.

Halfway through the crossing, the current grabbed the cub and carried him downstream. He became trapped in the small rapids at the bottom of the pool. There was little opportunity for swimming here. The calm water had suddenly turned fierce. Sometimes he was submerged, sometimes on the surface. He was constantly in turbulent motion, being flipped over or spun around, and repeatedly slammed against rocks. Each time he hit a rock, he cried out. His journey became a sequence of yelps, from which one could have counted the number of rocks he collided with.

Below the rapids lay a second pool, and here, caught by the swirling current, he was gently carried to the shore and softly placed on a bed of gravel. He scrambled desperately away from the water and collapsed. He had discovered something new about the world. Water wasn't alive, yet it moved. It also appeared as solid as the ground, but had no substance whatsoever. He concluded that things weren't always what they seemed to be. The cub's fear of the unknown came from an inherited wariness, and this experience had now made it stronger. From that point forward, by the very nature of things, he would carry with him a lasting suspicion of how things appeared. He would need to understand the true nature of something before he could trust it.

One more adventure awaited him that day. He suddenly remembered that somewhere in the world, his mother existed. Then a feeling washed over him that he needed her more than anything else in the entire world. His body wasn't just exhausted from all the adventures he had experienced, but his small mind was just as worn out. In all his days of life, his brain had never worked as intensely as it had this single day. On top of that, he felt drowsy. So he began searching for the cave and his mother, while being overwhelmed by crushing feelings of loneliness and helplessness.

He was moving through some bushes when he heard a sharp, threatening cry. A flash of yellow appeared before his eyes. He watched a weasel quickly leap away from him. It was a small living creature, and he felt no fear. Then, right in front of him at his feet, he spotted an extremely tiny living thing, only a few inches long—

a young weasel that, like him, had disobediently ventured out exploring. The little creature tried to back away from him. He flipped it over with his paw. It made a strange, scratching sound. The next moment the yellow flash appeared again before his eyes. He heard the threatening cry once more, and at that same instant felt a sharp strike on the side of his neck as the mother weasel's sharp teeth pierced his flesh.

While he yelped and cried out and scrambled backward, he saw the mother weasel leap upon her young one and disappear with it into the nearby thicket. The cut of her teeth in his neck still hurt, but his feelings were hurt more severely, and he sat down and weakly whimpered. This mother weasel was so small and so fierce. He had yet to learn that for size and weight the weasel was the most ferocious, vindictive, and terrible of all the killers of the wilderness. But a portion of this knowledge was quickly to be his.

He was still whimpering when the mother weasel came back. She didn't rush toward him now that her baby was safe. She moved forward more carefully, and the young wolf had plenty of time to watch her thin, snake-like body and her head, which stood upright, alert, and resembled a snake as well. Her sharp, threatening cry made the hair on his back stand up, and he growled at her in warning. She came nearer and nearer. There was a sudden leap, faster than his inexperienced eyes could follow, and the slender, yellow body vanished briefly from his sight. The next instant she was at his throat, her teeth sunk deep into his fur and skin.

At first he growled and attempted to fight back; but he was extremely young, and this was just his first day in existence, and his growl turned into a whimper, his fight became a struggle to get away. The weasel never loosened her grip. She held on, working to push down with her teeth to the major vein where his life-blood flowed. The weasel was a blood drinker, and it was always her preference to drink from the throat of life itself.

The gray cub would have died, and there would have been no story to tell about him, if the she-wolf hadn't come leaping through the bushes. The weasel released the cub and lunged at the she-wolf's throat, missing its target but managing to grab hold of her jaw instead. The she-wolf jerked her head with the force of a whip crack, breaking the weasel's grip and hurling it high into the air. And while it was still airborne, the she-wolf's jaws snapped shut on the thin, yellow body, and the weasel met its death between her crushing teeth.

The young wolf felt another wave of love from his mother. Her happiness at finding him appeared even stronger than his happiness at being discovered. She nuzzled him and stroked him and cleaned the wounds left by the weasel's bite. Afterward, the mother and her cub shared the blood-drinking creature as their meal, then returned to the cave where they rested.

Chapter V: The Law of Meat

The young wolf's growth was swift. He rested for two days, then ventured out from the cave once more. During this expedition, he discovered the young weasel whose mother he had helped devour, and he ensured that the young weasel met the same fate as its mother. However, on this journey he did not lose his way. When he became tired, he found his path back to the cave and slept. And each day after that saw him exploring outside and covering a larger territory.

He started to accurately assess his strengths and weaknesses, learning when to take risks and when to exercise caution. He discovered it was wise to remain cautious at all times, except during those rare instances when, confident in his own fearlessness, he gave in to minor fits of anger and desire.

He was always a fierce little devil whenever he came across a wandering ptarmigan. He never failed to react viciously to the chattering of the squirrel he had first encountered on that dead pine tree. Meanwhile, spotting a gray jay almost always sent him into an absolute fury, since he could never forget the sharp peck on his nose he had gotten from the first one of those birds he had met.

But there were moments when even a whiskey jack couldn't distract him, and these were moments when he sensed danger from some other roaming predator. He never forgot about the hawk, and whenever its shadow moved overhead, it always made him duck quickly into the closest brush. He no longer moved clumsily with his legs spread wide, and he was already beginning to develop his mother's way of walking—sneaky and secretive, seeming effortless, yet gliding forward with a speed that was as misleading as it was unnoticeable.

When it came to hunting for meat, all his good fortune had occurred at the very start. The seven young ptarmigan and the baby weasel made up the total of everything he had managed to kill. His urge to hunt grew stronger each day, and he developed fierce dreams of catching the squirrel that chattered so loudly and constantly warned every wild animal in the area that the wolf cub was coming near. However, since birds could fly through the sky and squirrels were able to climb trees, the cub could only attempt to creep up on the squirrel without being noticed when it happened to be on the ground.

The young wolf held deep respect for his mother. She had the ability to hunt and kill prey, and she consistently brought him his portion of the meal. Additionally, she showed no fear of anything around them. He didn't realize that her courage came from years of experience and accumulated wisdom. What he perceived was an aura of strength and dominance. His mother embodied power, and as he matured, he experienced this authority through the increasingly firm strikes of her paw, while the gentle corrective touch of her nose was replaced by the sharp bite of her teeth. This behavior also earned his respect. She demanded his compliance, and as he grew older, her patience with him grew thinner.

Famine returned, and the young wolf, now more aware than before, felt the sharp pangs of hunger once again. His mother grew gaunt as she searched desperately for food. She barely rested in the den anymore, dedicating nearly all her time to hunting for prey, though her efforts proved fruitless. While this period of starvation didn't drag on for long, it was brutal during its duration. The young wolf discovered that his mother's milk had dried up completely, and he didn't receive even a single bite of meat to sustain himself.

Before, he had hunted for fun, purely for the joy of it; now he hunted with deadly seriousness, and came up empty. Yet this failure sped up his growth. He observed the squirrel's behavior more carefully, and worked harder and more cleverly to sneak up on it and catch it off guard. He watched the wood-mice and attempted to dig them from their holes; and he discovered much about how moose-birds and woodpeckers lived. And a day arrived when the hawk's shadow no longer sent him cowering into the bushes. He had become stronger and smarter, and more sure of himself. He was also desperate. So he sat upright on his hind legs, clearly visible in an open area, and dared the hawk to come down from the sky. For he understood that there, soaring in the blue overhead, was food, the meat his belly craved so urgently. But the hawk wouldn't descend to fight, and the cub crawled back into a dense patch of brush and whined his frustration and hunger.

The famine ended. The she-wolf returned home with meat. This was unusual meat, unlike anything she had brought back before. It was a lynx kitten, partially grown, similar to the cub in size, but smaller. And it was entirely for him. His mother had already satisfied her hunger somewhere else; though he remained unaware that it was the remaining lynx litter that had satisfied her appetite. He also didn't understand the desperation behind her actions. He only understood that the soft-furred kitten was food, and he ate and grew more content with each bite.

A full belly leads to laziness, and the young wolf lay in the cave, sleeping pressed against his mother's side. Her snarling woke him up. He had never heard her snarl so fiercely before. This was probably the most terrifying snarl she had ever made in her entire life. She had good reason for it, and no one understood this better than she did. You don't raid a lynx's den without consequences. In the bright afternoon sunlight, crouched at the cave entrance, the cub spotted the mother lynx. The fur along his spine stood on end at the sight of her. This was pure fear, and he didn't need instinct to recognize it. Even if seeing her wasn't enough, the furious cry the intruder let out—starting as a snarl and suddenly rising into a harsh shriek—was convincing proof by itself.

The young wolf felt the surge of life within him and rose to his feet, snarling bravely beside his mother. However, she pushed him away shamefully and positioned him behind her. Due to the low entrance to their den, the lynx couldn't jump inside, and when it attempted a crawling attack, the female wolf leaped onto it and held it down. The cub witnessed only fragments of the fight. There was intense growling, spitting, and shrieking. Both creatures thrashed wildly, with the lynx slashing and clawing while also biting, whereas the female wolf relied solely on her teeth.

Once, the young wolf leaped forward and buried his teeth deep into the lynx's back leg. He held on tight, snarling fiercely. Without realizing it, his body weight hampered the leg's movement and prevented his mother from suffering worse injuries. A shift in the battle pinned him beneath both animals and forced him to let go. In the next instant, the two mothers broke apart, and before they charged at each other again, the lynx struck out at the cub with a massive front paw that tore his shoulder down to the bone and hurled him sideways into the wall. The cub's piercing cry of pain and terror now joined the chaos. However, the fight went on so long that he had enough time to exhaust his crying and find his courage returning; when the battle finally ended, he was once again gripping a back leg and growling ferociously through clenched teeth.

The lynx was dead. But the she-wolf was extremely weak and ill. Initially she nuzzled the cub and cleaned his injured shoulder with her tongue; however, the blood she had lost had drained away her strength, and for an entire day and night she remained beside her dead enemy's body, motionless, barely breathing. For a week she never ventured outside the cave, except to drink water, and even then her movements were sluggish and agonizing. By the end of that period the lynx had been completely consumed, while the she-wolf's injuries had healed enough to allow her to resume hunting for food once more.

The cub's shoulder remained stiff and painful, and he walked with a limp for quite some time due to the severe wound he had sustained. However, the world appeared different to him now. He moved through it with increased confidence, feeling a sense of strength and capability that hadn't existed before his fight with the lynx. He had witnessed life's more savage side; he had engaged in combat; he had sunk his teeth into an enemy's flesh; and he had lived through it all. Because of these experiences, he carried himself with greater boldness, displaying a hint of rebelliousness that was entirely new to his character. He no longer feared small matters, and much of his former shyness had disappeared, although the unknown continued to weigh on him with its secrets and dangers, invisible yet constantly threatening.

He started going with his mother on hunting trips, where he witnessed plenty of killing for food and began taking part in it himself. Through his own limited understanding, he grasped the fundamental rule of survival. There were two types of life—his own species and everything else. His own species consisted of his mother and himself. Everything else encompassed all living creatures that moved around. But everything else fell into different categories. One group represented what his own species hunted and consumed. This group was made up of creatures that didn't kill and smaller predators. The other group either killed and devoured his own species, or got killed and devoured by his own species. From this understanding came the fundamental rule. The purpose of existence was food. Life itself meant food. Living things survived by consuming other living things. There were those who ate and those who got eaten. The rule was simple: EAT OR BE EATEN. He didn't spell out this rule in precise, definite words or think deeply about its moral implications. He didn't even consciously consider the rule; he simply lived by it without any deliberate thought whatsoever.

He observed this natural law in action all around him. He had devoured the young ptarmigan chicks. The hawk had consumed the ptarmigan mother. That same hawk would have made a meal of him as well. Later, as he became stronger and more dangerous, he desired to kill and eat the hawk. He had consumed the lynx cub. The mother lynx would have devoured him if she hadn't been killed and eaten herself. This cycle continued endlessly. Every living creature around him was following this same law, and he was an integral part of it. He was a predator. His sole sustenance came from meat, living meat that either fled rapidly from his approach, took flight into the sky, scaled trees to escape, burrowed underground for safety, stood its ground to battle him, or reversed roles entirely and pursued him instead.

If the cub had been able to think like a human, he might have summed up life as nothing more than a ravenous hunger, and the world as a place where countless appetites roamed freely, chasing and being chased, hunting and being hunted, devouring and being devoured, all happening in darkness and bewilderment, filled with brutality and chaos, a complete mess of greed and killing, governed by random chance, without mercy, without purpose, without end.

The young wolf didn't think like humans do. He couldn't see the bigger picture or consider multiple perspectives. He focused on one thing at a time, driven by a single purpose or desire. Beyond the fundamental law of survival and hunting, countless other smaller rules governed his existence that he needed to discover and follow. His world overflowed with unexpected experiences. The vital energy coursing through him and the movement of his body brought him constant joy. Chasing down prey filled him with excitement and pure exhilaration. Even his fury and fights brought him satisfaction. Fear itself, along with the enigma of the unknown, gave meaning to his existence.

And there were comforts and pleasures. Having a full belly, dozing peacefully in the warm sunlight—these simple things were complete payment for all his struggles and hard work, while his efforts and labors were rewarding in themselves. They were expressions of life, and life is always joyful when it can express itself freely. So the young wolf had no complaints about his harsh surroundings. He was fully alive, deeply content, and filled with pride in himself.

Part III

Chapter I: The Makers of Fire

The young wolf stumbled across it without warning. The mistake was entirely his own. He had been reckless. He had abandoned the safety of the cave and rushed down to the water to quench his thirst. Perhaps he failed to pay attention because drowsiness weighed heavily upon him. (He had spent the entire night hunting for food, and had only recently stirred from sleep.) And his lack of caution might have stemmed from how well he knew the path to the watering hole. He had walked this route countless times, and nothing dangerous had ever occurred along the way.

He walked down past the dead pine tree, crossed the clearing, and jogged into the forest. At that exact moment, he both saw and caught the scent. In front of him, sitting quietly on their heels, were five living creatures unlike anything he had ever encountered before. This was his first sight of human beings. However, when they saw him, the five men didn't jump up, bare their teeth, or growl. They remained motionless, sitting there in threatening silence.

The cub remained completely still. Every natural instinct should have driven him to flee frantically, but suddenly, for the first time, a different and opposing instinct emerged within him. A profound sense of reverence overwhelmed him. He was paralyzed by an overpowering awareness of his own frailty and insignificance. Before him stood dominance and strength, something far beyond his understanding or capability.

The cub had never encountered a human being before, yet his instincts about humans were already there. In unclear ways, he recognized that humans were the creatures who had fought their way to dominance over all the other animals in the wilderness. The cub wasn't just seeing this human through his own eyes, but through the eyes of every ancestor that came before him—through eyes that had watched from the darkness around countless winter campfires, that had observed from safe distances and from deep within bushes at this strange, two-legged creature that ruled over all living things. The power of the cub's inherited nature controlled him, along with the fear and reverence that had developed over centuries of conflict and the combined experiences passed down through generations. This inheritance was too overwhelming for a wolf that was still just a cub. If he had been fully grown, he would have fled. Instead, he crouched down, frozen with terror, already beginning to offer the same surrender that his species had given from the very first time a wolf approached to sit beside a human's fire and feel its warmth.

One of the Native Americans stood up and walked toward him, then bent down over him. The young wolf pressed himself closer to the ground. This was the unknown made real at last, taking the form of actual flesh and blood, leaning over him and reaching down to grab him. His fur stood up on its own; his lips pulled back and his small fangs showed. The hand, hanging like fate above him, paused, and the man spoke with laughter, "Wabam wabisca ip pit tah." ("Look! The white fangs!")

The other Indians burst into laughter and encouraged the man to grab the cub. As his hand moved closer and closer, a fierce battle of instincts raged inside the young animal. Two powerful urges overwhelmed him—the desire to surrender and the need to fight back. What happened next was a mixture of both impulses. He submitted until the hand nearly made contact with him. Then he struck back, his teeth flashing as he snapped and bit down hard on the hand. In the next instant, he was struck on the side of his head, sending him tumbling onto his side. All his fighting spirit immediately vanished. His youth and natural instinct to submit took control of him. He sat back on his hind legs and whimpered loudly. However, the man who had been bitten was furious. The cub was hit on the opposite side of his head. This made him sit up and cry out even more loudly than before.

The four Indians burst into even louder laughter, and now even the man who had been bitten joined in their amusement. They gathered around the cub and mocked him as he cried out in terror and pain. Suddenly, in the middle of their laughter, he heard a sound. The Indians heard it as well. But the cub recognized what it was, and with one final, extended wail that carried more victory than sorrow, he stopped his crying and waited for his mother's arrival—his fierce and unconquerable mother who battled and destroyed everything in her path and knew no fear. She was growling as she raced toward them. She had heard her cub's distress call and was rushing to rescue him.

She leaped into their midst, her worried and fierce maternal instincts transforming her into anything but a beautiful creature. However, for the young wolf, witnessing her defensive fury brought him joy. He let out a happy little yelp and jumped toward her, while the humans quickly retreated several paces. The mother wolf positioned herself protectively over her offspring, confronting the men with raised fur and a growl rumbling deep within her chest. Her expression was twisted and threatening with danger, even the ridge of her nose creasing from tip to eyes, so intense was her snarl.

Then one of the men suddenly cried out. "Kiche!" he shouted. It was an exclamation of surprise. The cub felt his mother weakening at the sound.

"Kiche!" the man shouted again, this time with a sharp, commanding tone.

And then the young wolf saw his mother, the she-wolf, the fearless one, crouching down until her belly touched the earth, whimpering, wagging her tail, making gestures of peace. The cub couldn't comprehend what he was seeing. He was horrified. The overwhelming fear of humans washed over him once more. His instincts had been correct. His mother confirmed it. She, too, surrendered to the man-creatures.

The man who had spoken walked over to her. He placed his hand on her head, and she simply crouched down even lower. She didn't snap at him or show any signs of wanting to bite. The other men approached and gathered around her, touching and handling her, actions she made no effort to resist. They were very excited and made lots of sounds with their voices. These sounds weren't signs of danger, the cub determined, as he stayed crouched close to his mother, still bristling occasionally but trying his best to be submissive.

"It's not surprising," an Indian was saying. "Her father was a wolf. It's true, her mother was a dog; but didn't my brother tie her out in the woods for three full nights during mating season? That's why Kiche's father was a wolf."

"It's been a year, Grey Beaver, since she ran away," said a second Indian.

"It's not unusual, Salmon Tongue," Grey Beaver replied. "That was during the famine, and there wasn't any meat available for the dogs."

"She has lived with the wolves," said a third Indian.

"That appears to be the case, Three Eagles," Grey Beaver replied, placing his hand on the young wolf; "and this serves as proof of it."

The young wolf growled softly when the hand touched him, causing the hand to quickly pull back and deliver a sharp tap. As a result, the cub hid his teeth and crouched down in submission, while the hand came back to gently stroke behind his ears and along his back.

"This proves it," Grey Beaver continued. "It's clear that his mother is Kiche. But his father was a wolf. That's why there's little dog in him and much wolf. His fangs are white, and White Fang will be his name. I have spoken. He is my dog. Wasn't Kiche my brother's dog? And isn't my brother dead?"

The cub, who had now been given a name in the world, lay there watching. For a while the human beings continued making their vocal sounds. Then Grey Beaver pulled a knife from a sheath hanging around his neck and walked into the brush to cut a stick. White Fang observed him closely. He carved notches at both ends of the stick and secured strips of rawhide in the grooves. One strip he fastened around Kiche's throat. Then he led her to a small pine tree, where he tied the other strip around the trunk.

White Fang followed and lay down beside her. Salmon Tongue's hand reached out to him and rolled him over on his back. Kiche looked on anxiously. White Fang felt fear rising in him again. He couldn't quite hold back a snarl, but he made no attempt to bite. The hand, with fingers bent and spread apart, rubbed his stomach in a playful manner and rolled him from side to side. It was absurd and awkward, lying there on his back with legs sprawled in the air. Moreover, it was a position of such complete helplessness that White Fang's entire nature rebelled against it. He could do nothing to protect himself. If this man-creature meant harm, White Fang knew that he couldn't escape it. How could he leap away with his four legs in the air above him? Yet surrender made him control his fear, and he only growled quietly. This growl he couldn't hold back; nor did the man-creature punish it by striking him on the head. And furthermore, such was the oddness of it, White Fang experienced an unexplainable feeling of pleasure as the hand rubbed back and forth. When he was rolled on his side he stopped growling, when the fingers pressed and poked at the base of his ears the pleasant sensation grew stronger; and when, with a final rub and scratch, the man left him alone and went away, all fear had disappeared from White Fang. He would experience fear many times in his dealings with man; yet it was a sign of the fearless friendship with man that would eventually be his.

After some time, White Fang heard unfamiliar sounds drawing near. He quickly identified them, recognizing them immediately as the sounds made by humans. A few minutes later, the rest of the tribe, spread out in a long line as they traveled, arrived at the camp. The group included more men along with many women and children—forty people in total—all carrying heavy loads of camping gear and supplies. There were also numerous dogs, and except for the young puppies that weren't fully grown, these animals were also loaded down with camping equipment. Strapped securely to their backs in tightly fastened bags, the dogs each carried between twenty and thirty pounds.

White Fang had never encountered dogs before, but when he saw them he sensed they were his own species, though somehow different. However, they showed little distinction from wolves when they spotted the cub and his mother. There was a sudden charge. White Fang bristled and growled and snapped at the approaching wave of open-mouthed dogs rushing toward him, then fell beneath them, feeling the sharp cut of teeth piercing his body while he bit and clawed at the legs and stomachs above him. A tremendous commotion erupted. He could hear Kiche's snarling as she battled for him, and he could hear the shouts of the humans, the sound of clubs hitting bodies, and the cries of pain from the dogs that were struck.

Only a few seconds passed before he was back on his feet. He could now see the human beings driving the dogs away with clubs and stones, protecting him and saving him from the vicious teeth of creatures that were somehow like him but not truly his kind. And while his mind couldn't form a clear understanding of something as complex as justice, he still sensed, in his own way, the fairness of these human beings, and he recognized them for what they truly were—creators of rules and enforcers of those rules. He also recognized the power they wielded when carrying out these rules. Unlike any creatures he had ever met before, they didn't use their teeth or claws to fight. They strengthened their natural abilities by using inanimate objects. Lifeless things obeyed their commands. In this way, sticks and stones, controlled by these mysterious beings, flew through the air as if they were alive, causing serious injuries to the dogs.

To his mind, this represented extraordinary power—power that was unimaginable and beyond anything natural, power that seemed divine. White Fang, by his very nature, could never understand anything about gods; at most, he could only sense things that were beyond comprehension—but the wonder and reverence he felt for these man-animals was similar to the awe and amazement a human would experience upon seeing some heavenly being standing on a mountaintop, throwing lightning bolts from both hands at a stunned world.

The last dog had been forced to retreat. The commotion settled down. White Fang began licking his wounds and reflected on this experience—his first encounter with the cruelty of the pack and his initiation into pack life. He had never imagined that others like him existed beyond One Eye, his mother, and himself. They had formed their own separate group, and now, suddenly, he had found many more creatures that seemed to be of his own species. Deep down, he felt bitter that these others of his kind had immediately attacked him and attempted to kill him upon first sight. Similarly, he resented seeing his mother restrained by a rope, even though this was done by the superior human beings. It reminded him of being trapped, of captivity. However, he understood nothing about traps or captivity. The freedom to wander and run and rest wherever he chose had been his birthright, and now that freedom was being violated. His mother's movement was limited to the length of a rope, and he was equally confined by that same rope's length, since he still needed to stay close to his mother's side.

He didn't like it. He also didn't like it when the humans got up and continued their journey; a small human took the other end of the stick and led Kiche as a prisoner behind him, and behind Kiche followed White Fang, deeply troubled and anxious about this new experience he had gotten himself into.

They traveled down the stream's valley, venturing far beyond any territory White Fang had ever explored, until they reached the valley's end where the stream flowed into the Mackenzie River. At this location, where canoes hung suspended on tall poles and fish-drying racks stood ready for use, they established their camp, and White Fang observed everything with amazed eyes. These human creatures seemed more impressive with each passing moment. He witnessed their complete control over all the fierce-toothed dogs. This demonstrated raw power. Yet even more remarkable to the young wolf was their dominance over inanimate objects; their ability to make motionless things move; their power to transform the landscape itself.

It was this final sight that particularly struck him. The raising of wooden pole frameworks caught his attention; though this alone wasn't especially surprising, since it was accomplished by the same beings who hurled sticks and rocks across great distances. However, when these pole frameworks were transformed into tepees by draping them with fabric and animal hides, White Fang was amazed. What overwhelmed him was their enormous size. They sprang up all around him, surrounding him on every side, like some gigantic, rapidly sprouting form of life. They filled almost his entire field of view. They frightened him. They towered menacingly overhead; and when the wind caused them to sway with massive movements, he crouched low in terror, watching them cautiously, ready to leap away if they tried to collapse down on top of him.

But soon his fear of the tepees faded away. He watched women and children moving in and out of them safely, and he noticed dogs frequently trying to enter, only to be chased off with harsh words and thrown stones. Eventually, he left Kiche's side and crept carefully toward the wall of the closest tepee. It was the curiosity that comes with growing up that drove him forward—the need to learn and live and experience that brings knowledge. He covered the final few inches to the tepee wall with agonizing slowness and caution. The day's events had taught him that the unknown could reveal itself in the most incredible and unimaginable ways. Finally his nose made contact with the canvas. He waited. Nothing occurred. Then he sniffed the unfamiliar material, soaked with the scent of humans. He gripped the canvas between his teeth and pulled gently. Nothing occurred, though the nearby sections of the tepee shifted. He pulled harder. The movement increased. It was enjoyable. He pulled even harder, and again and again, until the entire tepee was swaying. Then a sharp shout from a woman inside sent him racing back to Kiche. But after that experience, he no longer feared the towering shapes of the tepees.

A moment later, he wandered away from his mother once more. Her stick was fastened to a stake in the ground, preventing her from following him. A half-grown puppy, considerably bigger and older than he was, approached him slowly with deliberate and aggressive arrogance. This puppy's name, as White Fang would later learn when he heard others call him, was Lip-lip. He had already experienced puppy fights and had become somewhat of a bully.

Lip-lip belonged to White Fang's own species, and since he was just a puppy, he didn't appear threatening; therefore White Fang got ready to greet him in a friendly manner. However, when the stranger's gait became rigid and his lips pulled back to expose his teeth, White Fang also tensed up and responded by baring his own teeth. They moved in half-circles around each other cautiously, growling and bristling with hostility. This continued for several minutes, and White Fang was starting to find it enjoyable, like some kind of game. But suddenly, with incredible speed, Lip-lip lunged forward, delivered a vicious bite, and quickly jumped back. The bite had struck the shoulder that the lynx had injured and that remained tender deep down near the bone. The shock and pain of the attack caused White Fang to cry out; but immediately afterward, filled with rage, he threw himself at Lip-lip and snapped ferociously.

But Lip-lip had spent his entire life in the camp and had been in countless puppy fights. Three times, four times, and half a dozen times, his sharp little teeth found their mark on the newcomer, until White Fang, crying out without shame, ran to seek safety with his mother. This was the first of many battles he would face against Lip-lip, for they were natural enemies from the very beginning, born with temperaments that would forever be in conflict.

Kiche gently licked White Fang with her tongue, trying to convince him to stay with her. However, his curiosity was overwhelming, and just a few minutes later he was setting off on another adventure. He encountered one of the human creatures, Grey Beaver, who was crouched down on his heels working with sticks and dry moss that he had laid out on the ground in front of him. White Fang approached him and observed. Grey Beaver made sounds with his mouth that White Fang understood as non-threatening, so he moved even closer.

Women and children were bringing more sticks and branches to Grey Beaver. This was clearly an important event. White Fang moved closer until he was touching Grey Beaver's knee, driven by curiosity and already forgetting that this was a fearsome human. Suddenly he noticed something strange like mist starting to rise from the sticks and moss under Grey Beaver's hands. Then, among the sticks themselves, a living thing appeared, twisting and turning, with a color like the sun in the sky. White Fang knew nothing about fire. It attracted him just as the light at the cave entrance had attracted him when he was a young puppy. He crawled several steps toward the flame. He heard Grey Beaver chuckle above him, and he recognized that the sound wasn't threatening. Then his nose touched the flame, and at that exact moment his little tongue reached out toward it.

For a moment he was frozen in place. The mysterious thing, hidden among the twigs and moss, was fiercely gripping his nose. He scrambled backwards, letting out a startled burst of yelping cries. When Kiche heard the sound, she sprang snarling to the limit of her rope, raging furiously because she couldn't reach him to help. But Grey Beaver roared with laughter, slapping his legs, and shared the story with everyone else in the camp until they were all laughing hysterically. Meanwhile, White Fang sat back on his hind legs, yelping and crying pitifully, a lonely and heartbreaking little creature surrounded by the human beings.

It was the most intense pain he had ever experienced. Both his nose and tongue had been burned by the living thing, bright as sunlight, that had sprung to life beneath Grey Beaver's hands. He whimpered and wailed without end, and each new cry brought fresh bursts of laughter from the humans. He attempted to comfort his nose with his tongue, but his tongue was also burned, and when the two injuries touched, they created even greater agony; this made him cry even more desperately and helplessly than before.

And then shame washed over him. He understood laughter and what it meant. We don't know how certain animals recognize laughter and realize when they're being mocked, but White Fang knew it in exactly the same way. He felt ashamed that these human creatures were laughing at him. He turned and ran away, not because of the pain from the fire, but because of the laughter that cut even deeper and wounded his very spirit. He fled to Kiche, who was thrashing wildly at the end of her rope like a crazed animal—to Kiche, the only being in the world who wasn't laughing at him.

Twilight faded and darkness settled in, with White Fang lying beside his mother. His nose and tongue were still sore, but a deeper problem troubled him. He missed home. He felt an emptiness inside himself, a longing for the peaceful silence of the stream and the cave in the rocky cliff. Life had become too crowded. There were too many humans—men, women, and children—all making sounds and causing disturbances. And there were the dogs, constantly fighting and arguing, breaking into loud outbursts and causing chaos. The peaceful solitude of the only life he had ever known was gone. Here the very air vibrated with activity. It hummed and buzzed without stopping. Constantly shifting in strength and suddenly changing in tone, it attacked his nerves and senses, made him anxious and restless and troubled him with the constant feeling that something was about to happen.

He watched the human beings coming and going and moving around the camp. In a way that distantly resembled how people look upon the gods they create, White Fang looked upon the human beings before him. They were superior creatures, truly, gods. To his limited understanding they were as much miracle-workers as gods are to people. They were creatures of control, possessing all kinds of unknown and impossible powers, rulers of the living and the non-living—making that which moved obey, giving movement to that which did not move, and making life, sun-colored and fierce life, to grow out of dead moss and wood. They were fire-makers! They were gods.

Chapter II: The Bondage

The days overflowed with new experiences for White Fang. While Kiche remained tethered by the stick, he roamed throughout the entire camp, exploring, examining, and discovering. He rapidly learned much about the behavior of the man-animals, but this growing familiarity didn't lead to scorn. The more he understood them, the more they proved their dominance, the more they revealed their enigmatic abilities, and the more their divine nature seemed to tower above him.

Humans often experience the sorrow of watching their gods fall from grace and their sacred places crumble to dust; but wolves and wild dogs that have come to lie at humanity's feet have never known this kind of heartbreak. Unlike humans, whose deities exist in the unseen and unknowable realm, existing as vapors and mists of imagination that slip away from any attempt to clothe them in reality, wandering spirits of longed-for virtue and strength, intangible extensions of the self reaching into the spiritual world— unlike humans, the wolf and wild dog that have approached the fire discover their gods in living, breathing flesh, solid to the touch, taking up physical space and needing time to achieve their purposes and sustain their existence. No leap of faith is required to believe in this kind of god; no amount of willpower could possibly create doubt about such a god's reality. There is no escaping it. There it stands, upright on two legs, weapon in hand, tremendously powerful, filled with passion and rage and love, deity and enigma and force all contained within flesh that bleeds when wounded and tastes good when eaten like any other meat.

And so it was with White Fang. The humans were clearly gods that could not be denied or avoided. Just as his mother, Kiche, had given her loyalty to them the moment they first called her name, he too was starting to give his loyalty. He granted them the right of way as something that undoubtedly belonged to them. When they walked, he moved out of their path. When they called, he came to them. When they made threats, he crouched down low. When they ordered him to leave, he hurried away. Behind every desire they had was the power to make that desire happen, power that could cause pain, power that showed itself through hits and beatings, through thrown rocks and the sharp sting of whip strikes.

He belonged to them just as all dogs belonged to them. His actions were theirs to control. His body was theirs to abuse, to trample on, to put up with. This was the lesson that quickly became clear to him. It was difficult to accept, since it went against much that was powerful and commanding in his own character; and, while he hated learning it, without realizing it he was beginning to enjoy it. It meant putting his fate in someone else's control, transferring the burdens of survival to others. This was actually a form of relief, because it's always simpler to depend on another person than to stand on your own.

But this complete surrender of himself, both physically and spiritually, to the human-animals didn't happen overnight. He couldn't instantly abandon his wild ancestry and his recollections of the wilderness. There were times when he would crawl to the forest's border and stand there, listening to something that beckoned him from distant places. And he would always come back, agitated and uneasy, to whine quietly and longingly beside Kiche, licking her face with his anxious, searching tongue.

White Fang quickly learned how life worked in the camp. He discovered the unfairness and selfishness of the older dogs whenever meat or fish was thrown out for them to eat. He began to understand that men were fairer, children were meaner, and women were kinder and more willing to throw him a piece of meat or a bone. And after experiencing two or three painful encounters with the mothers of half-grown puppies, he learned that it was always wise to leave these mothers alone, to stay as far away from them as he could, and to steer clear of them whenever he spotted them approaching.

But the curse of his existence was Lip-lip. Being bigger, older, and stronger, Lip-lip had chosen White Fang as his particular target for bullying. White Fang was ready to fight back, but he was completely outmatched. His opponent was simply too large. Lip-lip turned into a living nightmare for him. Every time he wandered away from his mother, the bully would inevitably show up, following close behind, growling at him, harassing him, and waiting for the perfect moment when no human was around to attack him and start a fight. Since Lip-lip always came out victorious, he took enormous pleasure in these encounters. It became his greatest source of joy in life, just as it became White Fang's greatest source of suffering.

But the impact on White Fang wasn't to intimidate him. Although he endured most of the injuries and was consistently beaten, his spirit stayed unbroken. However, a harmful consequence emerged. He grew bitter and sullen. His disposition had been fierce from birth, but it became even more ferocious under this constant torment. The friendly, playful, puppy-like aspect of his nature rarely showed itself. He never played or frolicked with the other young dogs in the camp. Lip-lip wouldn't allow it. The instant White Fang came near them, Lip-lip would attack him, intimidating and harassing him, or battling with him until he had chased him off.

The result of all this was that White Fang lost much of his puppyhood and began acting older than his actual age. Without the ability to release his energy through play, he turned inward and sharpened his mental abilities. He grew clever and cunning, spending his free time plotting and scheming. When the camp dogs were fed as a group, he was prevented from getting his fair share of meat and fish, so he became a skilled thief. He had to find food on his own, and he did so effectively, though this often made him a nuisance to the women of the camp. He learned to move quietly around the camp, to be sly and observant, to stay aware of everything happening around him, to watch and listen carefully, and to think strategically about how to successfully avoid his relentless tormentor.

It was early in the days of his torment that he played his first truly significant cunning game and experienced his first taste of vengeance. Just as Kiche, when she was with the wolves, had drawn unsuspecting dogs from human camps to their doom, so White Fang, in a somewhat similar fashion, lured Lip-lip into Kiche's vengeful jaws. Backing away from Lip-lip, White Fang made a roundabout escape that wound in and out and around the different tepees of the camp. He was a skilled runner, faster than any puppy his size, and faster than Lip-lip. But he didn't run at full speed during this pursuit. He barely maintained his lead, staying just one bound ahead of his chaser.

Lip-lip, thrilled by the pursuit and the constant closeness of his prey, lost sight of caution and his surroundings. By the time he realized where he was, it was already too late. Racing at full speed around a tepee, he crashed straight into Kiche who was lying at the end of her tether. He let out a single cry of alarm, and then her punishing jaws clamped down on him. She was restrained, but he couldn't escape from her grip easily. She knocked him off his feet so he couldn't run, while she continuously tore and cut him with her teeth.

When he finally managed to roll away from her, he struggled to his feet, completely disheveled and wounded both physically and emotionally. His fur stuck out in clumps all over his body where her teeth had torn at him. He stood where he had gotten up, opened his mouth, and let out a long, heartbroken puppy cry. But he wasn't even allowed to finish this. Halfway through his wail, White Fang charged in and sank his teeth into Lip-lip's back leg. Lip-lip had no fight left in him, and he ran away in disgrace, with his attacker close behind, harassing him all the way back to his own tepee. There the women came to help him, and White Fang, now transformed into a furious demon, was finally driven away only by a barrage of thrown stones.

The day arrived when Grey Beaver, convinced that the risk of her escaping had passed, set Kiche free. White Fang was thrilled by his mother's newfound freedom. He happily followed her around the camp, and as long as he stayed close beside her, Lip-lip maintained a cautious distance. White Fang even raised his hackles at him and strutted with rigid legs, but Lip-lip paid no attention to the provocation. He wasn't foolish either, and whatever revenge he wanted to take, he was willing to wait until he found White Fang by himself.

Later that day, Kiche and White Fang wandered to the edge of the forest beside the camp. He had guided his mother there, one step at a time, and now that she had stopped, he attempted to coax her further into the woods. The stream, the den, and the peaceful forest were beckoning to him, and he desperately wanted her to follow. He bounded forward a few steps, paused, and glanced back at her. She hadn't budged. He whimpered with longing and darted playfully in and out of the bushes. He raced back to her, licked her face, and bounded ahead once more. Still, she remained motionless. He stopped and stared at her, his entire body radiating intense focus and anticipation, but that energy slowly drained from him as she turned her head and looked back toward the camp.

There was something out in the wilderness calling to him. His mother could hear it as well. However, she also heard that other, stronger call—the call of fire and humanity, the call that among all creatures has been given only to the wolf to respond to, to the wolf and the wild dog, who share the same blood.

Kiche turned around and slowly jogged back toward the camp. More powerful than the physical control of the stick was the camp's hold on her. Invisible and mysteriously, the gods continued to maintain their grip with their strength and refused to release her.

White Fang sat down in the shade of a birch tree and whined quietly. There was an intense scent of pine, and delicate woodland aromas filled the air, bringing back memories of his former life of freedom before he became captive. However, he was still just a partially grown puppy, and more compelling than either the call of humans or the Wild was his mother's call. Throughout every hour of his brief existence, he had relied on her. The moment for independence had not yet arrived. Therefore, he stood up and sadly trotted back to the camp, stopping once and then again to sit down and whine and to hear the call that continued to echo from deep within the forest.

In the wilderness, a mother's time with her offspring is brief, but under human control it can be even briefer. This was White Fang's experience. Grey Beaver owed a debt to Three Eagles. Three Eagles was departing on a journey up the Mackenzie River to the Great Slave Lake. A piece of red cloth, a bear hide, twenty bullets, and Kiche were given to settle the debt. White Fang watched as his mother was placed in Three Eagles' canoe and attempted to follow her. A strike from Three Eagles sent him tumbling back onto the shore. The canoe pushed away from land. He leaped into the water and swam after it, ignoring Grey Beaver's harsh commands to come back. Even a human being, a god-like figure, White Fang disregarded, so great was his fear of losing his mother.

But gods expect to be obeyed, and Grey Beaver angrily pushed a canoe into the water to chase after him. When he caught up with White Fang, he reached down and grabbed him by the scruff of his neck, pulling him completely out of the water. He didn't immediately place him in the bottom of the canoe. Gripping him in the air with one hand, he used his other hand to beat him. And it was truly a beating. His hand was powerful. Each strike was calculated to cause pain; and he delivered countless blows.

Driven by the strikes that poured down on him from every direction, White Fang swayed back and forth like an unpredictable and unsteady pendulum. Different emotions swept through him in waves. Initially, he felt shock. Then brief terror washed over him, causing him to cry out repeatedly as the hand struck him. However, rage quickly replaced this fear. His wild instincts took control, and he bared his fangs and growled boldly at the furious god before him. This defiance only intensified the god's fury. The strikes came more rapidly, with greater force, and were more deliberately aimed to cause pain.

Grey Beaver kept beating him, and White Fang kept snarling. But this couldn't go on forever. One of them had to give up, and that one was White Fang. Fear rushed through him once more. This was the first time he was truly being overpowered by a human. The occasional hits from sticks and stones he had experienced before felt like gentle touches compared to this. He broke down and started to cry and whimper. For a while, each blow made him yelp; but his fear turned into terror, until eventually his cries came out in one continuous stream, no longer matching the timing of his punishment.

Finally, Grey Beaver stopped hitting him. White Fang hung loosely and kept whimpering. This appeared to please his master, who threw him down harshly into the bottom of the canoe. Meanwhile, the canoe had floated downstream. Grey Beaver grabbed the paddle. White Fang was blocking his path. He kicked him brutally with his foot. In that instant, White Fang's wild nature burst out once more, and he bit down on the moccasined foot.

The beating he had received earlier was nothing compared to what he endured now. Grey Beaver's fury was terrifying, and White Fang's terror was equally intense. Not only did the hand strike him, but the hard wooden paddle was also used against him, leaving him bruised and aching throughout his small body when he was thrown back into the canoe. Once more, and this time deliberately, Grey Beaver kicked him. White Fang did not attempt another attack on the foot. He had learned yet another harsh lesson about his captivity. Under no circumstances, regardless of the situation, could he ever dare to bite the god who ruled over him as lord and master. The body of his lord and master was sacred and must never be violated by the teeth of a creature like himself. This was clearly the worst of all crimes, the one transgression that could never be forgiven or ignored.

When the canoe reached the shore, White Fang lay whimpering and motionless, waiting for Grey Beaver's command. Grey Beaver wanted him to go ashore, so he was thrown onto the land, landing hard on his side and reopening his wounds. He shakily crawled to his feet and stood there whimpering. Lip-lip, who had been watching everything from the riverbank, immediately attacked him, knocking him down and biting into him. White Fang was too weak to fight back, and things would have gone badly for him if Grey Beaver hadn't kicked out with his foot, sending Lip-lip flying through the air with such force that he crashed to the ground a dozen feet away. This was the man-animal's sense of justice; and even in his own miserable condition, White Fang felt a small surge of gratitude. He limped obediently behind Grey Beaver through the village to the tepee. And that's how White Fang came to understand that the right to punish was something the gods kept for themselves and didn't allow the lesser creatures beneath them to have.

That night, when everything was quiet, White Fang thought about his mother and felt deep sadness for her. His grief was too loud and woke Grey Beaver, who struck him. From then on, he mourned quietly whenever the gods were nearby. However, sometimes when he wandered alone to the forest's edge, he released his sorrow and expressed it through loud whimpers and cries.

It was during this time that he could have listened to the memories of the den and the creek and returned to the wilderness. But the memory of his mother kept him there. Just as the hunting humans went out and came back, she would return to the village eventually. So he stayed in captivity, waiting for her.

But it wasn't entirely an unhappy form of captivity. There was plenty to capture his attention. Something was constantly occurring. The peculiar actions of these gods never ceased, and he remained eager to observe. Furthermore, he was discovering how to coexist with Grey Beaver. Complete, unwavering obedience was what was demanded from him; and in exchange he avoided beatings and his presence was accepted.

No, Grey Beaver himself would sometimes throw him a piece of meat and protect him from the other dogs while he ate it. Such a piece of meat held special value. In some mysterious way, it was worth more than a dozen pieces of meat from a woman's hand. Grey Beaver never petted or showed affection. Maybe it was the weight of his hand, maybe his fairness, maybe his raw power, or maybe it was all of these things that affected White Fang; because a certain bond of loyalty was developing between him and his stern master.

Gradually and through indirect means, as well as through physical force and violence, White Fang was being bound more tightly to his captivity. The traits that had originally allowed his species to approach human campfires were characteristics that could be cultivated and strengthened. These qualities were growing within him, and despite all its hardships, camp life was slowly becoming dear to him without his knowledge. However, White Fang remained completely unaware of this transformation. He experienced only sorrow over losing Kiche, hope that she would return, and an intense longing for the wild freedom he had once known.

Chapter III: The Outcast

Lip-lip kept making White Fang's life so miserable that White Fang became more vicious and cruel than he naturally should have been. While fierceness was part of his nature, the brutality that developed in him went far beyond what was natural. He gained a reputation for being troublesome among the humans themselves. Whenever there was chaos and commotion in the camp, fights and arguments, or the angry shouts of a woman discovering stolen meat, they could be certain to find White Fang involved in it and usually responsible for starting it. They didn't bother to investigate what caused his behavior. They only saw the results, and those results were terrible. He was sneaky and dishonest, a troublemaker who stirred up problems, and angry women would tell him directly to his face, while he watched them carefully and stayed ready to duck any object they might throw at him, that he was nothing but a wolf, completely worthless, and destined for a bad ending.

He became an outcast surrounded by the crowded camp. Every young dog in the pack followed Lip-lip's example. White Fang was different from the rest of them. Maybe they could sense his wilderness heritage and naturally felt the same hostility that domestic dogs have toward wolves. Whatever the reason, they all joined Lip-lip in tormenting him. Once they had turned against him, they discovered plenty of justification to keep opposing him. Each and every one of them experienced his bite at some point, and to his credit, he dealt out more punishment than he took. He could defeat many of them in one-on-one combat, but fair fights were never allowed. The moment any fight began, it became a signal for all the young dogs in camp to rush over and gang up on him.

From this group harassment, he discovered two crucial lessons: how to protect himself when facing multiple attackers at once, and how to cause maximum harm to a single opponent in the shortest possible time. Staying upright while surrounded by enemies was a matter of survival, and he mastered this skill completely. He developed feline-like agility in maintaining his balance. Even full-grown dogs could knock him backwards or to the side with the force of their massive bodies, and he would indeed be thrown backwards or sideways, whether airborne or skidding across the ground, but he always kept his legs beneath him and his paws pointing down toward the earth.

When dogs fight, there's typically some buildup before the real battle begins—growling, hair standing on end, and stiff-legged posturing. However, White Fang discovered how to skip these warning signs entirely. Any hesitation would result in all the young dogs ganging up on him. He had to strike fast and escape quickly. Therefore, he mastered the art of attacking without any signal of his plans. He would charge forward and bite and tear immediately, catching his opponent completely off guard before they could defend themselves. Through this approach, he discovered how to cause swift and serious injury. He also came to understand the power of catching an enemy unprepared. A dog caught defenseless, with its shoulder torn open or its ear shredded to pieces before it realized what was occurring, was already halfway defeated.

Moreover, it was surprisingly simple to knock down a dog that was caught off guard; when a dog was knocked down this way, it would always reveal for a brief moment the tender underside of its throat—the weak spot where a fatal blow could be delivered. White Fang understood this vulnerable point. This understanding had been passed down to him directly from generations of hunting wolves. Therefore, White Fang's strategy when he went on the attack was: first to locate a young dog by itself; second, to catch it unaware and knock it to the ground; and third, to strike quickly with his teeth at the exposed throat.

Since he was still only partially grown, his jaws hadn't yet developed enough size or strength to make his throat attacks fatal;

however, many young dogs wandered around the camp with torn throats as evidence of White Fang's deadly intentions. Then one day, when he caught one of his enemies alone at the forest's edge, he succeeded in killing the dog by repeatedly knocking him down and attacking his throat until he severed the major vein and drained the life from him. That night brought tremendous chaos. Someone had witnessed the attack, word had reached the dead dog's owner, the women recalled every instance of stolen meat, and Grey Beaver found himself surrounded by numerous furious voices. Nevertheless, he firmly guarded the entrance to his tepee, where he had secured the guilty party inside, and refused to allow the revenge that his fellow tribe members demanded.

White Fang became despised by both humans and dogs. Throughout this stage of his growth, he never experienced a single moment of safety. Every dog's fangs were turned against him, every person's hand raised in hostility. His own species welcomed him with growls, while his masters greeted him with harsh words and thrown rocks. He existed in constant tension. He remained perpetually on edge, watchful for any assault, cautious of potential attacks, keeping watch for sudden and unexpected projectiles, ready to react swiftly and with composure, to spring forward with bared teeth flashing, or to bound away while releasing a threatening growl.

When it came to snarling, he could snarl more fiercely than any dog in the camp, whether young or old. The purpose of a snarl is to warn or intimidate, and it takes good judgment to know when to use it. White Fang understood how to create this sound and when to deploy it. He put everything vicious, malicious, and terrifying into his snarl. With his nose wrinkled by constant spasms, his fur standing up in rolling waves, his tongue lashing out like a red snake before snapping back, his ears pressed flat, his eyes blazing with hatred, his lips pulled back, and his fangs bared and wet with saliva, he could force almost any attacker to hesitate. This brief pause, when his opponent was caught off guard, gave him the crucial moment he needed to think and decide what to do next. But often this pause stretched longer until it turned into a complete end to the attack. Against more than one of the adult dogs, White Fang's snarl allowed him to make a dignified retreat.

Rejected by the pack of adolescent dogs, White Fang's violent tactics and extraordinary skill forced the pack to suffer for their mistreatment of him. Since he wasn't allowed to run alongside the pack, a strange situation developed where no pack member could venture out alone. White Fang wouldn't allow it. Because of his ambush strategies and surprise attacks, the young dogs became too frightened to wander off by themselves. Except for Lip-lip, they were forced to stay clustered together for protection against the dangerous enemy they had created. A lone puppy near the riverbank meant either a dead puppy or one that would wake the entire camp with its piercing cries of pain and fear as it raced back from the wolf-cub that had attacked it.

But White Fang's revenge attacks didn't stop, even after the young dogs had completely learned that they needed to stick together. He would attack them whenever he found them alone, and they would attack him when they were grouped together. Just seeing him was enough to make them charge after him, and during these times his speed usually got him to safety. But trouble awaited any dog that ran faster than the others during such a chase! White Fang had learned to suddenly turn on the pursuer who was ahead of the pack and completely tear him apart before the rest of the pack could catch up. This happened very often, because once they were in full pursuit, the dogs tended to lose control of themselves in the thrill of the chase, while White Fang never lost control. Stealing quick looks behind him as he ran, he was always prepared to spin around and take down the overeager pursuer who had outrun his companions.

Young dogs naturally need to play, and given their circumstances, they turned their play into mock battles. This is how hunting White Fang became their main game—a dangerous game, nonetheless, and always a serious one. He, meanwhile, being the swiftest runner, wasn't afraid to go anywhere. During the time he waited uselessly for his mother's return, he led the pack on many wild chases through the surrounding forest. But the pack always lost track of him. Their noise and shouting alerted him to where they were, while he ran by himself, soft-footed, without sound, like a moving shadow between the trees in the same way his father and mother had done before him. Additionally, he had a stronger connection to the Wild than they did; and he understood more of its secrets and tactics. One of his favorite tricks was to disappear by running through water and then lie still in a nearby cluster of bushes while their confused howls echoed around him.

Despised by both his own species and humans, he remained unbreakable, constantly under attack while fighting his own endless battles, causing his growth to be swift but unbalanced. This environment offered no chance for gentleness and love to flourish. He possessed no understanding of such concepts whatsoever. The rules he absorbed were simple: submit to the powerful and dominate the vulnerable. Grey Beaver represented a deity, and he was strong. For this reason, White Fang followed his commands. However, any dog that was younger or smaller represented weakness, something that needed to be eliminated. His growth moved toward gaining power. To confront the relentless threat of injury and even death, his hunting and defensive abilities grew beyond normal limits. He developed faster reflexes than other dogs, greater speed, more cunning, increased lethality, enhanced agility, a leaner build with steel-like muscles and tendons, superior endurance, heightened cruelty, greater savagery, and sharper intelligence. He was forced to develop all these qualities, or he would not have maintained his position or survived in the harsh world where he lived.

Chapter IV: The Trail of The Gods

In the autumn, as the days grew shorter and the sharp chill of frost began to fill the air, White Fang found his opportunity for freedom. For many days, there had been tremendous activity throughout the village. The summer encampment was being taken apart, and the tribe was getting ready to depart with all their belongings for the autumn hunt. White Fang observed everything with keen eyes, and when the tepees started being taken down and the canoes were being loaded at the riverbank, he grasped what was happening. The canoes were already beginning to leave, and several had vanished down the river.

He made a deliberate decision to remain behind. He waited for the right moment to sneak away from camp into the forest. There, in the flowing stream where ice was starting to form, he concealed his tracks. Then he crept into the center of a thick grove of bushes and waited. Time went by, and he dozed on and off for hours. Eventually he was awakened by Grey Beaver's voice calling his name. Other voices could be heard as well. White Fang could make out Grey Beaver's wife joining in the search, along with Mit-sah, who was Grey Beaver's son.

White Fang shook with terror, and although he felt the urge to emerge from his hiding spot, he fought against it. Eventually the voices faded away, and sometime later he ventured out to savor the triumph of his escape. Night was approaching, and for a while he frolicked among the trees, delighting in his newfound freedom. Then, quite abruptly, he became conscious of his isolation. He settled down to think, listening to the forest's stillness and feeling troubled by it. The fact that nothing stirred or made a sound felt threatening. He sensed danger lurking nearby, invisible and unknown. He viewed the towering tree trunks with suspicion, along with the dark shadows that could hide all sorts of dangerous creatures.

Then the cold set in. There was no warm tepee wall to curl up against for comfort. Frost bit into his paws, and he found himself constantly lifting one front foot, then the other. He wrapped his thick, bushy tail around to shield them, and as he did, a vision appeared before him. Nothing unusual about it—just a series of memory images flashing across his mind's eye. He could see the camp once more, the tepees standing tall, the crackling fires blazing bright. The sharp voices of the women reached his ears, along with the deep, rumbling tones of the men and the growling of the dogs. Hunger gnawed at him, and he recalled the scraps of meat and fish that people used to toss his way. But here there was no food, nothing except a menacing and unforgiving silence.

His captivity had made him soft. Being free from responsibility had weakened him. He had lost the ability to take care of himself. The night stretched endlessly around him. His senses, used to the noise and activity of the camp, accustomed to the constant bombardment of things to see and hear, now had nothing to occupy them. There was nothing to do, nothing to see or hear. They struggled to detect any break in the silence and stillness of nature. They were horrified by the lack of activity and by the sense that something dreadful was about to happen.

He jumped with a sudden burst of terror. An enormous and shapeless form was racing across what he could see. It turned out to be the shadow of a tree cast by the moon, which had emerged as the clouds cleared away from its surface. Feeling relieved, he let out a quiet whimper; then he quickly stifled the sound, worried that it might draw the attention of whatever threats were hiding nearby.

A tree, shrinking in the cool night air, made a loud crack. It was right above him. He cried out in terror. Panic gripped him, and he ran frantically toward the village. He felt an overwhelming need for human protection and companionship. The scent of campfire smoke filled his nostrils. The sounds and voices of the camp echoed loudly in his ears. He emerged from the forest into the moonlit clearing where there were no shadows or darkness. But no village met his gaze. He had forgotten. The village was gone.

His frantic escape came to a sudden halt. There was nowhere left to run. He crept miserably through the abandoned camp, catching the scent of garbage piles and the thrown-away scraps and remnants left by the gods. He would have welcomed the clatter of rocks hurled at him by a furious woman, would have been grateful for Grey Beaver's hand striking him in anger; he would have greeted Lip-lip and the entire growling, cowardly pack with joy.

He arrived at the spot where Grey Beaver's tepee had been standing. In the middle of the area where it had been located, he settled down. He lifted his nose toward the moon. His throat seized up with tight spasms, his mouth fell open, and in a heartbroken wail poured out his loneliness and terror, his sorrow for Kiche, all his previous pain and suffering along with his dread of the hardships and perils that lay ahead. It was the extended wolf-howl, deep and sorrowful, the first howl he had ever made.

The arrival of daylight drove away his fears but made his loneliness even more intense. The bare ground, which just moments before had been filled with life, forced his isolation upon him with greater intensity. It didn't take him much time to decide what to do. He dove into the forest and followed the riverbank downstream. He ran all day without stopping. He didn't pause to rest. He appeared built to run indefinitely. His steel-strong body paid no attention to exhaustion. And even when weariness finally set in, his inherited stamina strengthened him for limitless effort and allowed him to push his aching body forward.

Where the river curved sharply against steep cliffs, he climbed the towering mountains that rose behind them. He crossed or swam through the rivers and streams that flowed into the main waterway. Frequently he traveled on the thin ice that was starting to form along the edges, and several times he broke through and fought desperately for his life in the freezing current. He constantly watched for any sign of the gods' trail where it might turn away from the river and head into the interior.

White Fang possessed intelligence that surpassed most of his species, but his mental capacity wasn't broad enough to consider the opposite shore of the Mackenzie River. The thought that his masters' trail might continue on the far side never occurred to him. Perhaps in time, after more travel and with the wisdom that comes with age, after learning more about trails and waterways, he might develop the ability to understand and consider such a possibility. However, that level of mental development lay ahead in his future. At this moment, he ran without such reasoning, focusing his thoughts solely on his own side of the Mackenzie.

All night he ran, stumbling through the darkness into accidents and barriers that slowed him down but didn't break his spirit. By the middle of the second day he had been running without stopping for thirty hours, and his body's strength was failing. It was his mental determination that kept him moving forward. He hadn't eaten in forty hours, and hunger was making him weak. The constant soaking in the freezing water had also taken its toll on him. His beautiful coat was matted and wet. The thick pads of his feet were bruised and bleeding. He had started to limp, and this limp got worse as the hours passed. To make matters worse, the sky darkened and snow began to fall—a cold, wet, melting, sticky snow that was slippery beneath his feet, hiding the landscape he traveled through and covering the uneven ground so that each step became more difficult and painful.

Grey Beaver had planned to set up camp that night on the far side of the Mackenzie River, since that's where the best hunting could be found. However, on the near side of the river, just before darkness fell, Kloo-kooch, who was Grey Beaver's wife, spotted a moose coming down to the water to drink. If the moose hadn't come down to drink, if Mit-sah hadn't steered off course because of the snow, if Kloo-kooch hadn't seen the moose, and if Grey Beaver hadn't killed it with a fortunate shot from his rifle, everything that followed would have unfolded very differently. Grey Beaver wouldn't have made camp on the near side of the Mackenzie, and White Fang would have continued past and moved on, either to perish or to find his way back to his wild brothers and join them—remaining a wolf for the rest of his life.

Night had fallen. The snow was coming down more heavily, and White Fang, whimpering quietly to himself as he stumbled and limped forward, discovered a fresh trail in the snow. It was so recent that he recognized it instantly for what it was. Whining with excitement, he followed it back from the riverbank and into the trees. The sounds of the camp reached his ears. He saw the glow of the fire, Kloo-kooch cooking, and Grey Beaver crouching on his heels and chewing a piece of raw fat. There was fresh meat in camp!

White Fang anticipated a beating. He crouched down and his fur stood on end slightly as he thought about it. Then he moved forward once more. He was afraid of and hated the beating he knew awaited him. However, he also understood that the warmth of the fire would be his, along with the protection of the gods and the company of the dogs—the latter being a hostile companionship, but companionship nonetheless and one that fulfilled his need to be part of a group.

He approached cringing and crawling into the firelight. Grey Beaver noticed him and stopped chewing the tallow. White Fang crawled slowly, cringing and groveling in complete humiliation and submission. He crawled directly toward Grey Beaver, each inch of his movement becoming slower and more agonizing. Finally he lay at his master's feet, surrendering himself completely into Grey Beaver's possession, willingly giving up both body and soul. By his own decision, he came to sit beside man's fire and be governed by him. White Fang shook, waiting for punishment to strike him. There was movement from the hand above him. He flinched instinctively, expecting the blow. It never came. He stole a quick look upward. Grey Beaver was breaking the chunk of tallow in half! Grey Beaver was offering him a piece of the tallow! Very carefully and with some suspicion, he first sniffed the tallow and then began to eat it. Grey Beaver commanded that meat be brought to him, and protected him from the other dogs while he ate. Afterward, grateful and satisfied, White Fang lay at Grey Beaver's feet, staring at the fire that warmed him, blinking and drowsing, confident in knowing that tomorrow would find him not wandering alone through harsh forest wilderness, but in the camp of the man-animals, with the gods to whom he had surrendered himself and on whom he now relied.

Chapter V: The Covenant

When December was well underway, Grey Beaver embarked on a journey up the Mackenzie River. Mit-sah and Kloo-kooch accompanied him on the trip. He drove one sled himself, pulled by dogs he had either traded for or borrowed from others. Mit-sah operated a second, smaller sled, which was pulled by a team of young puppies. The setup was more like a plaything than anything serious, but it brought Mit-sah tremendous joy, as he felt he was starting to contribute real work like a grown man. Additionally, he was gaining experience in handling and training dogs, while the puppies were getting accustomed to wearing harnesses and pulling loads. Beyond that, the sled served a practical purpose, as it transported nearly two hundred pounds of supplies and food.

White Fang had watched the camp dogs working in their harnesses, so he didn't resist too much when the harness was first put on him. A collar stuffed with moss was placed around his neck, and it was connected by two pulling straps to a band that went around his chest and over his back. The long rope he used to pull the sled was attached to this harness.

There were seven puppies on the team. The other dogs had been born earlier that year and were nine and ten months old, while White Fang was only eight months old. Each dog was attached to the sled with a single rope. No two ropes were the same length, and the difference in length between any two ropes was at least the length of a dog's body. Every rope was connected to a ring at the front of the sled. The sled itself had no runners, being a birch-bark toboggan with an upturned front end to prevent it from diving under the snow. This design allowed the weight of the sled and its load to be spread across the largest possible snow surface, since the snow was like crystal powder and very soft. Following the same principle of distributing weight as widely as possible, the dogs at the ends of their ropes spread out in a fan shape from the front of the sled, ensuring that no dog stepped in another's tracks.

There was also another advantage to the fan-shaped formation. The ropes of different lengths stopped the dogs from attacking those running ahead of them from behind. If a dog wanted to attack another, it would need to turn on one connected to a shorter rope. When this happened, it would come face to face with the dog it was attacking, and it would also have to deal with the driver's whip. However, the most unusual benefit of all was that any dog trying to attack one running in front of it had to pull the sled more quickly, and the faster the sled moved, the quicker the attacked dog could escape. Therefore, the dog behind could never catch the one ahead. The harder it ran, the faster the one it was chasing ran, and the faster all the dogs ran. At the same time, the sled moved more rapidly, and in this way, through clever indirect methods, humans strengthened their control over these animals.

Mit-sah looked like his father and had inherited much of his father's gray wisdom. In earlier times, he had watched Lip-lip torment White Fang, but back then Lip-lip belonged to another man, so Mit-sah had never dared do more than throw an occasional stone at him. Now, however, Lip-lip was his dog, and he set out to get his revenge by placing him at the end of the longest rope. This position made Lip-lip the leader, which seemed like an honor, but in reality it stripped him of all true honor, and instead of being the bully and master of the pack, he now found himself despised and tormented by the other dogs.

Because he ran at the end of the longest rope, the dogs always saw him running away ahead of them. All they could see of him was his bushy tail and his fleeing back legs—a sight much less fierce and threatening than his bristling mane and gleaming fangs. Also, since dogs are naturally wired this way mentally, seeing him run away made them want to chase after him and gave them the impression that he was fleeing from them.

The moment the sled began moving, the team chased after Lip-lip in a pursuit that lasted the entire day. Initially, he had been inclined to turn on his pursuers, protective of his pride and filled with rage; but during these moments Mit-sah would crack the sharp lash of the thirty-foot caribou-gut whip across his face and force him to turn around and keep running. Lip-lip could confront the pack, but he couldn't face that whip, and all he could do was keep his long rope tight and stay ahead of his teammates' snapping teeth.

But an even more clever strategy was hidden deep within the Indian's thinking. To make the endless chase of the leader more intense, Mit-sah treated him better than the other dogs. This special treatment filled them with jealousy and anger. When they were all together, Mit-sah would give meat to him and only to him. This drove them crazy with rage. They would circle around furiously just beyond the reach of the whip, while Lip-lip ate the meat and Mit-sah stood guard over him. And when there was no meat available, Mit-sah would keep the team at a distance and pretend to give meat to Lip-lip.

White Fang adapted well to the work. He had traveled a much greater distance than the other dogs in surrendering himself to the authority of the gods, and he had learned far more completely how pointless it was to resist their commands. Furthermore, the harassment he had endured from the pack had diminished the pack's importance to him in the order of things, while increasing man's significance. He had never learned to depend on his own species for friendship. Moreover, Kiche was almost entirely forgotten; and the primary way he could still express himself was through the loyalty he offered to the gods he had come to accept as his masters. Therefore he worked diligently, acquired discipline, and remained obedient. Devotion and eagerness defined his labor. These are fundamental qualities of the wolf and the wild dog once they have been tamed, and White Fang displayed these characteristics to an extraordinary degree.

A relationship did exist between White Fang and the other dogs, but it was one of conflict and hostility. He had never learned to play with them. He only knew how to fight, and fight with them he did, paying them back a hundred times over for all the bites and cuts they had given him back when Lip-lip was the pack leader. But Lip-lip was no longer the leader—except when he ran away from his teammates at the end of his rope, with the sled bouncing along behind him. In camp he stayed close to Mit-sah or Grey Beaver or Kloo-kooch. He didn't dare wander away from the gods, because now all the dogs had turned their fangs against him, and he experienced the full bitter taste of the persecution that had once been White Fang's burden.

After defeating Lip-lip, White Fang could have taken control of the pack as its leader. However, he was too gloomy and withdrawn for such a role. He simply beat up his teammates when necessary. Beyond that, he paid them no attention. The other dogs moved out of his path whenever he approached, and even the bravest among them never dared to steal his food. Instead, they ate their own meals quickly, worried that he might snatch their food away. White Fang understood the natural order perfectly: dominate those weaker than you and submit to those who are stronger. He consumed his portion of meat as fast as possible. And then trouble awaited any dog that hadn't finished eating yet! With a growl and a quick flash of his teeth, that unfortunate dog would howl its protests to the indifferent stars above while White Fang polished off the remaining food.

Every now and then, though, one dog or another would burst into rebellion and quickly get put down. This kept White Fang in fighting shape. He was protective of the separation he maintained within the pack, and he frequently fought to preserve it. However, these battles didn't last long. He moved too fast for the other dogs. They found themselves cut open and bleeding before they realized what was happening, defeated almost before they had even started fighting.

White Fang maintained discipline among his pack with the same unwavering strictness as the gods controlled their sleds. He never gave them any freedom or flexibility. He forced them to show him constant respect. They could behave however they wanted with each other. That wasn't his business. But he made it his business to ensure they left him alone in his solitude, moved out of his path when he chose to walk through their group, and always recognized his dominance over them. The slightest sign of defiance from them—a stiff posture, a raised lip, or bristling fur—and he would attack them without mercy or compassion, quickly teaching them they had made a mistake.

He was a brutal tyrant. His control was as unyielding as steel. He crushed the weak without mercy. It wasn't without reason that he had been subjected to the merciless battles for survival during his early days as a cub, when he and his mother, isolated and without help, managed to hold their ground and endure in the savage world of the wilderness. And it wasn't without purpose that he had mastered the art of moving carefully when faced with greater power. He dominated the weak, but he showed respect to the strong. And throughout the extended journey with Grey Beaver, he moved with great caution among the adult dogs in the camps of the unfamiliar human beings they came across.

The months went by. Grey Beaver's journey continued without end. White Fang grew stronger from the long hours on the trail and the constant work pulling the sled, and it appeared that his mental growth was nearly finished. He had learned to understand completely the world where he lived. His view of life was harsh and cold. The world he experienced was savage and cruel, a place without warmth, a place where gentle touches and love and the joyful pleasures of the soul had no place.

White Fang felt no love for Grey Beaver. Yes, Grey Beaver was like a god to him, but he was a cruel and harsh god. White Fang willingly accepted Grey Beaver's authority over him, but this authority came from Grey Beaver's superior intelligence and raw physical power. Something deep within White Fang's very nature made him want to submit to this leadership—otherwise, he wouldn't have returned from the wilderness when he did to offer his loyalty. There were hidden depths in his character that had never been explored or understood. A gentle word or a loving touch from Grey Beaver might have reached into those depths, but Grey Beaver never showed affection or spoke with kindness. That simply wasn't his nature. His dominance was brutal, and he ruled with brutality, delivering justice with a club, punishing wrongdoing with painful blows, and rewarding good behavior not through kindness, but simply by choosing not to strike.

So White Fang had no idea about the kindness that a human hand could offer him. Moreover, he didn't trust the hands of these human creatures. He remained wary of them. While it was true that sometimes they provided food, more frequently they caused pain. Hands were something to avoid at all costs. They threw rocks, swung sticks and clubs and whips, delivered slaps and blows, and when they made contact with him, they were clever at inflicting pain through pinching and twisting and pulling. In unfamiliar settlements he had come across the hands of children and discovered that they were merciless in causing harm. Additionally, he had once almost lost an eye to a stumbling young child. Through these encounters he grew distrustful of all children. He couldn't stand being around them. Whenever they approached with their threatening hands, he would stand up.

It was in a village at Great Slave Lake that White Fang came to change the law he had learned from Grey Beaver while dealing with the cruelty he faced from humans: the unforgivable sin was biting one of the gods. In this village, White Fang went searching for food, just as all dogs do in every village. A boy was chopping frozen moose meat with an axe, and the pieces were scattering in the snow. White Fang, moving quietly as he looked for meat, stopped and started eating the scattered pieces. He noticed the boy put down the axe and pick up a heavy club. White Fang jumped away, barely escaping the club as it came down toward him. The boy chased after him, and White Fang, being a stranger in the village, ran between two tepees only to find himself trapped against a tall dirt wall.

White Fang had nowhere to run. The only escape route lay between the two tepees, and the boy blocked that path. Gripping his club and ready to strike, he closed in on his trapped prey. White Fang was enraged. He confronted the boy, his fur standing on end as he growled and snarled, his sense of fairness violated. He understood the rules of scavenging. All the scraps of meat, including the frozen pieces, belonged to whichever dog discovered them. He had committed no crime, violated no rule, yet here stood this boy, preparing to beat him. White Fang barely understood what took place next. He acted in a burst of fury. And he moved so swiftly that the boy couldn't comprehend it either. All the boy realized was that he had somehow been knocked backward into the snow, and that White Fang's teeth had torn his club-wielding hand wide open.

But White Fang understood that he had violated the divine law. He had sunk his teeth into the sacred flesh of one of the gods, and he could expect nothing less than severe punishment. He ran to Grey Beaver, crouching behind his protective legs when the injured boy and his family arrived, demanding revenge. However, they departed without getting their satisfaction. Grey Beaver stood up for White Fang. Mit-sah and Kloo-kooch did the same. White Fang, hearing the heated argument and observing the furious gestures, realized that his actions were warranted. Through this experience, he discovered that there were different types of gods. There were his own gods, and there were foreign gods, and a clear distinction existed between them. Whether it involved fairness or unfairness, it made no difference—he had to accept everything that came from his own gods. However, he wasn't obligated to tolerate mistreatment from the other gods. It was his right to respond with his teeth. This, too, was part of divine law.

Before the day ended, White Fang would learn even more about this law. Mit-sah was alone in the forest collecting firewood when he ran into the boy who had been bitten. Several other boys were with him. Angry words were exchanged. Then all the boys ganged up on Mit-sah. Things were going badly for him. He was getting hit from every direction. At first, White Fang just watched. This was a matter between the gods and had nothing to do with him. Then he realized this was Mit-sah, one of his own special gods, who was being attacked. White Fang didn't think through what he did next—it wasn't a calculated decision. A wild surge of rage sent him charging into the fight. Five minutes later, boys were running away in all directions across the landscape, many of them leaving drops of blood on the snow as proof that White Fang's teeth had been busy. When Mit-sah told everyone back at camp what had happened, Grey Beaver commanded that meat be given to White Fang. He ordered a large amount of meat to be given, and White Fang, stuffed full and drowsy by the fire, understood that the law had been proven true.

Through these experiences, White Fang learned about property rights and his responsibility to protect what belonged to his master. Moving from guarding his god's body to defending his god's belongings was a natural progression, and he made this transition easily. Everything that belonged to his god needed protection from everyone else—even if it meant biting other gods. Such behavior wasn't just disrespectful by nature, but it was also extremely dangerous. The gods possessed overwhelming power, and a dog couldn't possibly win against them in a fight; however, White Fang learned to confront them with fierce aggression and without fear. His sense of duty overcame his fear, and the thieving gods eventually learned to stay away from Grey Beaver's belongings.

One thing White Fang learned quickly in this situation was that a god who steals is usually a coward and tends to flee when an alarm is raised. He also discovered that only a short time passed between when he sounded the alarm and when Grey Beaver arrived to help him. White Fang came to understand that it wasn't fear of him that made the thief run away, but rather fear of Grey Beaver. White Fang didn't raise the alarm by barking. He never barked. His approach was to charge directly at the intruder and bite them if possible. Because he was gloomy and preferred to be alone, having no interaction with the other dogs, he was particularly well-suited to protect his master's belongings; Grey Beaver encouraged and trained him in this role. One consequence of this was that White Fang became more fierce and stubborn, and even more isolated.

The months passed, strengthening the bond between dog and man more and more. This was the ancient agreement that the first wolf to leave the wilderness had made with humanity. And, just like all the wolves and wild dogs that followed after, White Fang figured out this agreement on his own. The conditions were straightforward. In exchange for having a living, breathing god, he gave up his freedom. Food and warmth, safety and friendship were among the benefits he gained from his god. In exchange, he protected the god's belongings, defended his body, labored for him, and followed his commands.

The possession of a god requires service. White Fang's service was one of duty and reverence, but not of love. He didn't understand what love was. He had no experience with love. Kiche remained only a distant memory. Furthermore, he had not only left behind the wilderness and his own kind when he surrendered himself to humans, but the conditions of this agreement meant that even if he encountered Kiche again, he wouldn't abandon his god to follow her. His loyalty to humans felt like a fundamental law of his existence that was stronger than his love of freedom, his species, and his family.

Chapter VI: The Famine

Spring was approaching when Grey Beaver completed his lengthy journey. It was April, and White Fang had reached one year of age when he arrived at the home villages and Mit-sah released him from the harness. Although he was still far from being fully grown,

White Fang was the largest yearling in the village, second only to Lip-lip in size. He had inherited his height and strength from both his father, the wolf, and from Kiche, and he was already comparable in size to the adult dogs. However, he had not yet developed a compact build. His frame was lean and lanky, and his strength was more wiry than solid. His fur displayed the authentic wolf-grey coloring, and in every way he appeared to be a genuine wolf. The small portion of dog ancestry he had inherited from Kiche had left no physical trace on him, although it had influenced his psychological development.

He walked through the village, feeling a calm sense of satisfaction as he recognized the different gods he had known before his long journey. There were also the dogs—puppies that had grown up just as he had, and adult dogs that didn't seem as big and intimidating as he remembered them. He also felt less afraid of them than he used to, moving among them with a relaxed confidence that was both new to him and pleasant.

There was Baseek, a weathered old dog who in his earlier years only needed to bare his teeth to make White Fang cower and retreat in submission. White Fang had discovered much about his own powerlessness from this dog, and now he would learn just as much about the transformation and growth that had occurred within himself. While Baseek had grown weaker with advancing age, White Fang had grown stronger with his youth.

It was while butchering a freshly killed moose that White Fang discovered how his relationship with the other dogs had changed. He had claimed a hoof and part of the leg bone for himself, with a good amount of meat still clinging to it. He had moved away from the chaotic feeding frenzy of the pack—actually hiding behind some bushes where they couldn't see him—and was enjoying his prize when Baseek charged at him. Before White Fang realized what he was doing, he had struck the intruder twice with his teeth and leaped back out of reach. Baseek was shocked by

White Fang's boldness and lightning-fast counterattack. He stood there, staring blankly at White Fang across the distance, the bloody, raw leg bone lying between them.

Baseek was old, and he had already learned about the growing courage of the dogs he used to intimidate. These were painful lessons that he was forced to accept, drawing on all his experience to deal with them. In earlier times, he would have attacked White Fang in a rage of justified anger. But now his declining strength wouldn't allow him to take such action. He bristled aggressively and stared threateningly across the shin-bone at White Fang. And White Fang, bringing back quite a bit of his old fear, appeared to weaken and shrink into himself and become smaller, as he searched his mind for a way to retreat without losing too much dignity.

And this is exactly where Baseek made his mistake. If he had simply maintained his fierce and threatening appearance, everything would have worked out fine. White Fang, who was already on the edge of backing down, would have withdrawn and left the meat for him. However, Baseek couldn't wait. He assumed the victory was already his and moved toward the meat. When he carelessly lowered his head to sniff it, White Fang's fur bristled slightly. Even at that moment, Baseek still had a chance to salvage the situation. If he had just positioned himself over the meat with his head raised and glaring menacingly, White Fang would have eventually crept away. But the scent of fresh meat filled Baseek's nostrils powerfully, and his hunger drove him to take a bite.

This was more than White Fang could tolerate. Coming fresh off months of dominating his own pack mates, his self-control couldn't handle watching another dog eat the meat that rightfully belonged to him. He attacked in his usual way, without any warning. His first strike tore Baseek's right ear to shreds. Baseek was shocked by how suddenly it happened. But even more devastating things were occurring just as quickly. He got knocked to the ground. White Fang bit his throat. As Baseek tried to get back on his feet, the younger dog buried his teeth into his shoulder twice. The speed of the attack left him completely confused. He made a desperate lunge at White Fang, but his jaws snapped at nothing but air. An instant later, his nose was split open, and he found himself stumbling backward, away from the meat.

The roles had completely switched. White Fang now stood guard over the shin-bone, his fur bristling with threat and aggression, while Baseek positioned himself at a distance, getting ready to back down. He didn't dare engage in combat with this young streak of lightning, and once again he experienced, more painfully than before, the weakness that came with advancing years. His effort to preserve his dignity was courageous. Coolly turning his back on both the young dog and the bone, as if neither deserved his attention or was worth his time, he walked away with stately pride. Only after he was completely out of view did he pause to tend to his bleeding injuries.

The impact on White Fang was to instill in him greater confidence and increased pride. He moved with less caution among the adult dogs; his behavior toward them became less yielding. This didn't mean he actively sought out conflict. Quite the opposite. However, as he went about his business, he expected respect. He insisted on his right to move freely without interference and refused to step aside for any dog. He demanded to be acknowledged, nothing more. He would no longer be overlooked and dismissed, which was the fate of puppies, and which remained the fate of the puppies who were his teammates. They moved out of the way, yielded the path to the adult dogs, and surrendered their food to them when forced. But White Fang, unsociable, isolated, sullen, barely glancing left or right, formidable, intimidating in appearance, distant and foreign, was recognized as an equal by his bewildered seniors. They rapidly discovered it was best to avoid him, neither attempting aggressive actions nor offering gestures of friendship. If they kept their distance from him, he kept his distance from them—an arrangement that they discovered, after several confrontations, to be extremely preferable.

In midsummer White Fang had an experience. Moving quietly along in his usual silent manner to examine a new tepee that had been set up at the village's edge while he was away hunting moose with the hunters, he suddenly encountered Kiche face to face. He stopped and gazed at her. He recalled her dimly, but he did recall her, which was more than she could say about him. She curled her lip at him with the familiar threatening snarl, and his memory sharpened. His long-forgotten puppyhood, everything connected to that recognizable snarl, flooded back to him. Before he had discovered the gods, she had been the center of his entire world. The old familiar emotions from that time returned to him, welling up inside him. He leaped toward her with joy, and she greeted him with sharp fangs that sliced his cheek down to the bone. He couldn't comprehend what had happened. He retreated, confused and perplexed.

But this wasn't Kiche's fault. A wolf mother isn't designed to remember her cubs from a year or so earlier. So she had no memory of White Fang. He was an unfamiliar animal, a trespasser; and her current litter of puppies gave her every right to resent such an intrusion.

One of the puppies crawled over to White Fang. The two were half-brothers, though neither of them realized it. White Fang sniffed at the puppy with curiosity, which caused Kiche to attack him immediately, slashing his face for the second time. He retreated even further back. All the ancient memories and feelings faded away once more and returned to the depths from which they had briefly emerged. He watched Kiche as she licked her puppy, pausing occasionally to growl menacingly at him. She meant nothing to him now. He had discovered how to survive without her. Her significance had been erased from his mind. There was no room for her in his world, just as there was no room for him in hers.

He remained there, confused and disoriented, his memories wiped away, trying to understand what was happening, when Kiche launched a third attack against him, determined to drive him completely away from the area. White Fang let himself be forced to retreat. This was a female of his species, and it was a natural law among his kind that males must never fight females. He didn't understand this law intellectually, since it wasn't something he had reasoned out or learned through worldly experience. He felt it as an inner compulsion, as an instinctive drive—the same instinct that made him howl at the moon and stars during the night, and that filled him with fear of death and the unknown.

The months passed. White Fang became stronger, heavier, and more solid, while his personality developed according to the patterns established by his genetics and surroundings. His genetic makeup was like raw material that could be compared to clay. It held many potential outcomes and could be shaped into numerous different forms. His environment acted as the sculptor of this clay, giving it a specific shape. Therefore, if White Fang had never encountered the campfires of humans, the wilderness would have shaped him into a genuine wolf. However, the gods had placed him in a different environment, and he was molded into a dog that retained wolf-like qualities, but remained a dog rather than a wolf.

Based on his natural temperament and the harsh conditions around him, his personality was gradually taking on a specific form. This transformation was inevitable. He was growing increasingly gloomy, less sociable, more isolated, and more savage; meanwhile, the dogs were discovering that maintaining peace with him was far wiser than engaging in conflict, and Grey Beaver was beginning to value him more highly as time went on.

White Fang, despite appearing to possess strength in every aspect of his character, had one persistent flaw that plagued him. He couldn't tolerate being the target of laughter. When men laughed, it filled him with hatred. They could laugh amongst themselves about whatever they wanted, as long as it wasn't about him, and this didn't bother him at all. However, the instant their laughter focused on him, he would explode into an absolutely furious rage. Though he was typically serious, dignified, and solemn, laughter would drive him to a state of wild absurdity. It infuriated and disturbed him so deeply that he would act like a wild beast for hours afterward. Any dog unlucky enough to cross his path during these episodes was in serious trouble. He understood the rules too well to take his anger out on Grey Beaver; Grey Beaver had both a club and divine authority backing him. But the other dogs had nothing protecting them except empty space, and they would flee into that space whenever White Fang appeared, driven to madness by laughter.

In the third year of his life, a severe famine struck the Mackenzie Indians. During the summer, the fish disappeared. When winter arrived, the caribou abandoned their usual migration routes. Moose became rare, rabbits nearly vanished entirely, and both hunting animals and their prey died off. Deprived of their normal food sources and weakened by starvation, they turned on each other for survival. Only the strongest managed to live through it. White Fang's gods were perpetual hunters. The elderly and frail among them starved to death. Cries of anguish echoed throughout the village, where women and children went hungry so that their meager supplies could feed the gaunt, sunken-eyed hunters who wandered through the forest in their futile search for meat.

The gods reached such desperate conditions that they consumed the soft-tanned leather from their moccasins and mittens, while the dogs devoured the harnesses from their backs and even the whip-lashes. Furthermore, the dogs began eating each other, and the gods also ate the dogs. Those who were weakest and least valuable were consumed first. The surviving dogs watched and comprehended what was happening. A handful of the most courageous and intelligent abandoned the gods' fires, which had transformed into a slaughterhouse, and escaped into the forest, where they eventually starved to death or were killed by wolves.

During this difficult time, White Fang also slipped away into the forest. He was better suited for this kind of life than the other dogs because his early training as a cub served as his guide. He became particularly skilled at hunting small creatures. He would remain hidden for hours, watching every move of a wary tree squirrel, waiting with patience as enormous as the hunger that gnawed at him, until the squirrel dared to come down to the ground. Even at that moment, White Fang didn't act too quickly. He waited until he was certain he could strike before the squirrel could reach the safety of a tree. Only then would he burst from his hiding spot like a gray missile, impossibly fast, never missing his target—the escaping squirrel that simply couldn't run fast enough.

Successful as he was with squirrels, there was one difficulty that prevented him from living and growing fat on them. There weren't enough squirrels. So he was forced to hunt even smaller creatures. His hunger became so intense at times that he would dig out wood mice from their underground burrows. He didn't hesitate to fight with a weasel that was just as hungry as he was and far more vicious.

During the most desperate times of the famine, he crept back to the fires of the gods. However, he didn't approach the fires directly. He hid in the forest, staying out of sight and stealing from the traps whenever game was occasionally caught. He even took a rabbit from Grey Beaver's snare at a time when Grey Beaver stumbled and swayed through the forest, frequently sitting down to rest due to his weakness and difficulty breathing.

One day White Fang came across a young wolf that was thin and bony, its joints loose from starvation. If White Fang hadn't been hungry himself, he might have traveled with the wolf and eventually discovered his place within the pack among his wild relatives. Instead, he chased down the young wolf, killed it, and ate it.

Fortune appeared to smile upon him. Whenever he was most desperately in need of food, he managed to find something to hunt and kill. Similarly, during his weakest moments, luck ensured that none of the larger predatory animals discovered him. Therefore, he had gained strength from two days of feeding on a lynx when a starving wolf pack charged straight at him. The pursuit was long and merciless, but he was better fed than his pursuers, and ultimately he outran them. Not only did he escape them, but by making a wide circle back along his own trail, he caught one of his exhausted hunters.

After that, he left that region and traveled to the valley where he had been born. There, in the familiar den, he found Kiche. True to her old ways, she had also escaped the unwelcoming fires of the gods and returned to her former shelter to give birth to her offspring. When White Fang arrived, only one from this litter was still alive, and this one wasn't meant to survive much longer. Young life had little opportunity in such severe hunger.

Kiche's welcome to her adult son was far from loving. However, White Fang wasn't bothered by this. He had grown beyond needing his mother. So he calmly turned around and continued trotting upstream. When he reached the fork in the stream, he took the left path, which led him to the lynx's den where he and his mother had battled long ago. There, in the deserted den, he made himself comfortable and rested for a day.

During the early summer, in the final days of the famine, he encountered Lip-lip, who had also retreated to the woods, where he had managed to scrape together a wretched existence.

White Fang encountered him without warning. Moving in opposite directions along the bottom of a tall cliff, they came around a rocky corner and suddenly found themselves facing each other. Both stopped immediately with alarm and eyed each other with suspicion.

White Fang was in excellent shape. His hunting had been successful, and for a week he had eaten until he was completely satisfied. He was still full from his most recent kill. But the moment he saw Lip-lip, his fur stood up all along his back. This bristling happened without his control, a physical reaction that had always occurred in the past when Lip-lip's bullying and harassment created that familiar mental state in him. Just as he had bristled and growled at the sight of Lip-lip before, he now bristled and growled automatically. He didn't hesitate. The attack was swift and decisive. Lip-lip tried to retreat, but White Fang slammed into him hard, shoulder against shoulder. Lip-lip was knocked down and tumbled onto his back. White Fang's teeth sank into the thin throat. A death struggle followed, during which White Fang circled around, his legs stiff and his eyes watchful. Then he continued on his way and trotted along the bottom of the cliff.

One day, not long after, he reached the edge of the forest, where a narrow strip of open land sloped down to the Mackenzie River. He had traveled over this ground before when it was empty, but now a village sat there. Still concealed among the trees, he stopped to examine the situation. The sights, sounds, and smells were familiar to him. It was the old village relocated to a new spot. But the sights, sounds, and smells were different from what he had last experienced when he had run away from it. There was no whimpering or wailing. Pleasant sounds reached his ears, and when he heard the angry voice of a woman, he recognized it as the anger that comes from having a full belly. And there was the smell of fish in the air. There was food. The famine had ended. He emerged boldly from the forest and trotted into the camp straight to Grey Beaver's tepee. Grey Beaver wasn't there, but Kloo-kooch greeted him with joyful cries and an entire fresh-caught fish, and he lay down to wait for Grey Beaver's return.

Part IV

Chapter I: The Enemy of His Kind

If White Fang had ever possessed any chance, however slight, of eventually forming bonds with other dogs, that possibility was completely destroyed when Mit-sah made him the lead dog of the sled team. The other dogs now despised him—they hated him for the extra food Mit-sah gave him; they resented all the real and imagined special treatment he received; they loathed him because he always ran at the front of the team, with his bushy tail waving and his constantly retreating hindquarters forever taunting them.

White Fang returned their hatred with equal intensity. Being the lead dog brought him no satisfaction whatsoever. Having to flee from the howling pack—every single dog he had beaten and dominated for three years—was nearly unbearable. Yet he had to endure it or die, and his life force refused to give up. The instant Mit-sah commanded them to start, the entire team lunged toward White Fang with eager, fierce barks.

There was no way for him to defend himself. If he turned to face them, Mit-sah would crack the stinging whip across his face. His only option was to run away. He couldn't confront that howling pack with his tail and hindquarters exposed. These were hardly adequate weapons to face so many ruthless fangs. So he ran, betraying his own nature and pride with every stride he took, and he kept running all day long.

You can't go against your natural instincts without having those instincts turn back on you. This kind of backlash is like a hair that's supposed to grow outward from the skin but instead curves back unnaturally and grows into the body—creating a painful, infected wound. This is exactly what happened to White Fang. Every fiber of his being urged him to attack the pack that howled behind him, but the gods' will forbade this; and to back up that will, there was the caribou-hide whip with its stinging thirty-foot lash. So White Fang could only consume himself with bitterness and nurture a hatred and spite that matched the wildness and stubborn strength of his nature.

If there was ever a creature that stood as the enemy of its own species, White Fang was exactly that creature. He never asked for mercy and never showed any. The pack's teeth constantly left him wounded and scarred, while he just as consistently marked them with his own bites. Most lead dogs, when camp was set up and they were freed from their harnesses, would stay close to their human masters for safety. White Fang scorned such protection. He roamed the camp fearlessly, delivering nighttime punishment for the suffering he had endured during the day. Before he became the team's leader, the pack had learned to stay out of his path. Now things were different. Stirred up by chasing him all day long, unconsciously influenced by the repeated image burned into their minds of him running away, and driven by the sense of dominance they had felt throughout the day, the dogs couldn't make themselves step aside for him anymore. Whenever he appeared among them, a fight would break out. His movement through the camp was accompanied by snarling, snapping, and growling. The very air around him was thick with hatred and spite, which only fed the hatred and spite growing inside him.

When Mit-sah shouted his command for the team to halt, White Fang followed orders. Initially this created problems with the other dogs. They would all attack the despised leader only to discover the situation had reversed. Mit-sah would be standing behind him, the powerful whip crackling in his grip. Eventually the dogs learned that when the team stopped on command, White Fang was to be left alone. However, when White Fang stopped without being ordered to do so, they were permitted to attack him and kill him if possible. After going through this several times, White Fang never stopped unless commanded. He was a fast learner. Given the circumstances, he had to learn rapidly if he wanted to survive the exceptionally harsh conditions that governed his existence.

But the dogs could never learn to leave him alone in camp. Each day, as they chased him and barked their defiance, they forgot the previous night's lesson, and that night would have to teach them all over again, only to be immediately forgotten once more. Beyond this, their dislike of him ran much deeper. They sensed a fundamental difference between themselves and him— reason enough for their hostility. Like him, they were domesticated wolves. But they had been tamed for generations. Much of the wilderness had been bred out of them, so that to them the wild represented the unknown, the terrifying, the ever-threatening and ever-hostile force. But he still carried the wild within him, in his appearance, his actions, and his instincts. He embodied it, served as its living representation: so when they bared their teeth at him, they were protecting themselves against the destructive forces that lurked in the forest shadows and in the darkness beyond the campfire's glow.

But the dogs did learn one important lesson, and that was to stick together. White Fang was too dangerous for any of them to confront alone. They faced him as a group, because otherwise he would have killed them one by one in a single night. As things stood, he never got the opportunity to kill them. He might knock a dog down, but the pack would attack him before he could follow through and deliver the fatal bite to the throat. At the first sign of trouble, the entire team would unite and confront him. The dogs had their own fights with each other, but these disputes were set aside whenever White Fang posed a threat.

On the other hand, no matter how hard they tried, they couldn't kill White Fang. He was too fast for them, too dangerous, too clever. He stayed away from confined spaces and always retreated whenever they seemed likely to surround him. As for knocking him down, there wasn't a single dog among them that could pull it off. His paws gripped the ground with the same determination that he held onto life. In this endless battle with the pack, staying upright and staying alive meant the same thing, and nobody understood this better than White Fang.

So he became the enemy of his own species, these domesticated wolves that had grown soft by human fires and weak under the protective shelter of human strength. White Fang was filled with bitterness and showed no mercy. This was how his nature had been shaped. He declared war against all dogs. He carried out this war so ruthlessly that Grey Beaver, savage though he was himself, couldn't help but be amazed by White Fang's brutality. Never before, he declared, had there been an animal like this one; and the Native Americans in distant villages made the same declaration when they heard the stories of the dogs he had killed among theirs.

When White Fang was nearly five years old, Grey Beaver took him on another long journey, and he would always remember the destruction he caused among the dogs in the many villages along the Mackenzie, across the Rockies, and down the Porcupine to the Yukon. He delighted in the revenge he took on his own kind. These were ordinary, unsuspecting dogs. They weren't ready for his speed and directness, for his sudden attacks without any warning. They didn't understand what he truly was—a lightning bolt of death. They would approach him with bristled fur, walking stiffly and ready to challenge him, while he wasted no time with fancy displays, springing into action like a steel coil, going straight for their throats and killing them before they realized what was happening and while they were still shocked by surprise.

He became skilled at fighting. He conserved his energy. He never squandered his strength, never struggled unnecessarily. He moved in too fast for that, and if he failed to connect, he retreated just as quickly. The wolf's aversion to close combat was his to an extraordinary extent. He couldn't tolerate extended contact with another body. It felt dangerous. It drove him wild. He had to get away, break free, stand on his own feet, not touching any living creature. It was the wilderness still holding onto him, expressing itself through him. This sensation had been intensified by the outcast life he had lived since he was a puppy. Danger hid in physical contact. It was the snare, always the snare, the dread of it lurking deep within his very existence, woven into his essence.

As a result, the unfamiliar dogs he came across stood no chance against him. He avoided their teeth. He defeated them or escaped, remaining unharmed in both situations. Naturally, there were occasional exceptions to this pattern. Sometimes multiple dogs would attack him at once and hurt him before he could escape; other times a lone dog would manage to wound him badly. However, these incidents were rare accidents. For the most part, he had become such a skilled fighter that he traveled without injury.

Another advantage he had was his ability to accurately judge time and distance. He didn't do this deliberately, though. He never calculated these things. Everything happened automatically. His eyes perceived things correctly, and his nervous system transmitted these images accurately to his brain. His body parts functioned better than those of an ordinary dog. They operated together more fluidly and consistently. He possessed superior nervous, mental, and physical coordination. When his eyes sent his brain the moving picture of an action, his brain instinctively understood the space that contained that action and how long it would take to complete. Because of this, he could dodge another dog's leap or avoid its snapping teeth, while simultaneously finding that tiny moment needed to launch his own attack. His body and mind formed a more refined machine. This wasn't something he deserved credit for. Nature had simply been more generous with him than with the typical animal, nothing more.

White Fang reached Fort Yukon during the summer months. Grey Beaver had traveled across the massive watershed that separates the Mackenzie and Yukon rivers during late winter, then spent the spring hunting in the western foothills of the Rocky Mountains. After the ice broke up on the Porcupine River, he constructed a canoe and paddled downstream to the point where it meets the Yukon River, just south of the Arctic Circle. The old Hudson's Bay Company fort was located there, along with many Native Americans, abundant food supplies, and extraordinary excitement. This was the summer of 1898, when thousands of prospectors were heading up the Yukon River toward Dawson and the Klondike. Though they were still hundreds of miles away from their destination, many of these gold seekers had already been traveling for an entire year, and the shortest distance anyone had covered to reach that point was five thousand miles, while others had journeyed from the opposite side of the globe.

Here Grey Beaver came to a halt. Word of the gold rush had reached him, and he had arrived carrying several bundles of furs, along with another bundle of gut-sewn mittens and moccasins. He wouldn't have risked such an extensive journey if he hadn't anticipated substantial profits. However, what he had anticipated was nothing compared to what he actually achieved. His most ambitious expectations had never gone beyond a hundred percent profit; he earned a thousand percent. And like a genuine Indian, he prepared to conduct business methodically and patiently, even if it required the entire summer and the remainder of the winter to sell all his merchandise.

It was at Fort Yukon that White Fang encountered his first white men. Compared to the Indians he had known, they seemed like an entirely different race of beings, a race of superior gods.

They struck him as having greater power, and power is what godhood is built upon. White Fang didn't think this through logically, nor did he form a clear conclusion in his mind that the white gods were more powerful. This was simply a feeling, nothing more, yet it was no less compelling. Just as the towering shapes of the tepees, built by human hands, had impressed him as displays of power during his puppyhood, so now he was affected by the houses and the massive fort constructed entirely of heavy logs. Here was power. These white gods were strong. They had greater control over the physical world than the gods he had known, the most powerful of whom was Grey Beaver. Yet Grey Beaver seemed like a child-god compared to these white-skinned ones.

Certainly, White Fang only experienced these emotions. He wasn't aware of them consciously. However, animals usually act based on feelings rather than thoughts, and every action White Fang took now stemmed from his sense that the white men were superior beings. First of all, he was extremely wary of them. There was no way to know what mysterious dangers they possessed or what unknown pain they might inflict. He wanted to watch them but was afraid they might notice him. During the first few hours, he was satisfied with creeping around and observing them from a safe distance. Then he noticed that the dogs near them weren't being harmed, so he moved closer.

In return, he became a source of intense fascination for them. His wolf-like looks immediately captured their attention, and they gestured toward him while speaking to each other. This pointing made White Fang wary, and whenever they attempted to come closer, he bared his teeth and retreated. None of them managed to touch him, which was fortunate for everyone involved.

White Fang quickly discovered that only a small number of these gods—no more than twelve—actually lived at this location. Every few days, a steamboat (another massive display of power) would arrive at the riverbank and remain there for several hours.

White men would disembark from these steamboats and later board them again to leave. There appeared to be countless numbers of these white men. During his first day or two there, he observed more of them than he had encountered Indians throughout his entire life; and as time passed, they kept arriving by river, making brief stops, and then continuing upstream until they disappeared from view.

But if the white gods were all-powerful, their dogs weren't particularly impressive. White Fang quickly figured this out when he encountered the dogs that came ashore with their masters. These dogs came in all sorts of odd shapes and sizes. Some had legs that were far too short, while others had legs that were far too long. Instead of proper fur, they had hair, and some barely had any hair at all. Most importantly, none of them had any idea how to fight.

As an enemy of his species, White Fang's role was to battle against them. He did exactly that, and he rapidly developed tremendous disdain for them. They were weak and defenseless, created a lot of racket, and stumbled about awkwardly attempting to achieve through brute force what he accomplished through skill and cleverness. They charged at him with loud roars. He leaped to one side. They had no idea where he had gone; and in that instant he attacked them at the shoulder, knocking them down and striking at their throat.

Sometimes this attack worked, and an injured dog would roll in the dirt, only to be jumped on and ripped apart by the pack of Indian dogs that stood waiting. White Fang had learned to be smart. He had figured out long ago that the gods became furious when their dogs were killed. The white men were just the same in this regard. So when he had knocked down one of their dogs and slashed its throat wide open, he was satisfied to step back and let the pack move in to do the brutal final work. That's when the white men would charge in, unleashing their fury on the pack, while White Fang escaped punishment. He would position himself at a safe distance and watch as stones, clubs, axes, and all kinds of weapons rained down on his fellow dogs. White Fang had become very smart indeed.

But his companions became clever in their own way, and White Fang learned alongside them. They discovered that their best opportunity for excitement came when a steamboat first docked at the riverbank. Once the first two or three unfamiliar dogs had been attacked and killed, the white men quickly herded their own animals back onto the vessel and unleashed brutal revenge on those responsible. One white man, after watching his dog—a setter—get torn apart right in front of him, pulled out a revolver. He shot quickly, firing six rounds, and six members of the pack fell dead or dying—yet another display of power that made a lasting impression on White Fang's mind.

White Fang found great pleasure in all of this. He felt no affection for his own species, and he was clever enough to avoid getting hurt himself. Initially, killing the white men's dogs had simply been entertainment. Eventually, it became his main activity. He had no other work to occupy his time. Grey Beaver was occupied with trading and accumulating wealth. Therefore, White Fang spent his time at the landing with the dishonorable pack of Indian dogs, waiting for steamers to arrive. When a steamer pulled in, the excitement would begin. Within a few minutes, once the white men had recovered from their shock, the pack would disperse. The excitement was finished until the next steamer would come.

But it would be difficult to say that White Fang was truly part of the pack. He didn't mix with the other dogs, instead keeping his distance, always maintaining his independence, and the pack actually feared him. It's true that he collaborated with them. He would start fights with unfamiliar dogs while the pack stood by and watched. And after he had defeated the strange dog, the pack would move in to finish the job. But it's just as true that he would then pull back, leaving the pack to face the anger and punishment of the furious gods.

It didn't take much effort to start these fights. All he had to do when the unfamiliar dogs came to shore was reveal himself. The moment they spotted him, they charged at him. This was their natural instinct. He represented the Wild—the unknown, the fearsome, the constantly threatening force that had stalked through the shadows around the fires of the ancient world when they huddled close to those flames, transforming their instincts and learning to dread the Wild from which they had emerged, and which they had abandoned and turned against. Through countless generations, this terror of the Wild had been embedded deep within their very nature. For hundreds of years, the Wild had symbolized fear and devastation. Throughout this entire period, their masters had given them complete freedom to destroy anything that belonged to the Wild. By doing so, they had safeguarded both themselves and the gods whose fellowship they enjoyed.

And so, coming straight from the gentle southern regions, these dogs walked down the gangplank and stepped onto the Yukon shore, needing only to catch sight of White Fang to feel an overwhelming urge to attack and kill him. They may have been city-bred dogs, but they still possessed that primal fear of the wilderness. They didn't just see this wolf-like creature with their own eyes as he stood before them in broad daylight. They viewed him through the eyes of their forebears, and through their inherited memories they recognized White Fang as a wolf, recalling the age-old conflict between their kinds.

All of this made White Fang's days pleasant and satisfying. If seeing him caused these unfamiliar dogs to attack him, that worked out well for him and badly for them. They viewed him as fair game for hunting, and he saw them the same way.

It wasn't by chance that he had first opened his eyes in an isolated den and battled his earliest fights against ptarmigan, weasels, and lynx. And it wasn't by accident that his early months had been filled with suffering from Lip-lip's cruelty and the harassment of the entire puppy pack. Things could have unfolded differently, and he would have developed differently as a result. If Lip-lip had never existed, he would have spent his youth playing with the other puppies and matured to be more dog-like with a greater fondness for other dogs. If Grey Beaver had possessed the depth of tenderness and love, he might have explored the hidden depths of White Fang's character and drawn out all sorts of gentle traits. But circumstances had not aligned that way. White Fang's character had been shaped until he became exactly what he was: sullen and isolated, incapable of love and savage, hostile toward all members of his species.

Chapter II: The Mad God

A small group of white men lived in Fort Yukon. These men had spent many years in the region. They called themselves Sourdoughs and took enormous pride in this classification. They felt nothing but contempt for other men who were new to the territory. The men who disembarked from the steamboats were newcomers. They were called cheechakos, and they always cringed when this term was applied to them. They baked their bread using baking powder. This was the unfavorable distinction that separated them from the Sourdoughs, who made their bread from sourdough starter simply because they had no access to baking powder.

All of this was beside the point. The men stationed at the fort looked down on the new arrivals and took pleasure in watching them struggle. They particularly enjoyed the chaos that White

Fang and his unruly pack caused among the newcomers' dogs. Whenever a steamboat pulled in, the fort's men made sure to head down to the riverbank to watch the entertainment unfold. They awaited these moments with the same eager excitement as the Indian dogs, and they were quick to admire the fierce and cunning role that White Fang played in it all.

But there was one man among them who especially loved this brutal entertainment. He would come running at the first sound of a steamboat's whistle, and when the final fight ended and White Fang and the pack had dispersed, he would walk slowly back to the fort, his expression heavy with disappointment. Sometimes, when a gentle southern dog fell, screaming its death cry beneath the fangs of the pack, this man couldn't control himself and would jump into the air, shouting with joy. And he always watched White Fang with keen, greedy eyes.

The other men at the fort called this man "Beauty." Nobody knew what his real first name was, and throughout the region people generally knew him as Beauty Smith. However, he was far from beautiful. His nickname came from irony. He was remarkably ugly. Nature had been stingy when creating him. He started out as a small man, and on top of his thin body sat an even more noticeably thin head. The top of his head could be compared to a sharp point. Actually, during his childhood, before his companions had given him the nickname Beauty, they used to call him "Pinhead."

From the back, starting at the top of his head, his skull angled downward to his neck, and from the front it sloped sharply to meet a low but unusually broad forehead. Starting at this point, as if making up for her earlier stinginess, Nature had generously distributed his facial features. His eyes were enormous, with the space of two full eyes between them. His face was massive compared to the rest of his body. To accommodate all these features, Nature had equipped him with a huge jutting jaw. It was broad and thick, extending outward and downward until it appeared to be resting against his chest. This effect might have been caused by his thin neck being too weak to properly hold up such a heavy load.

This jaw created an impression of fierce determination. However, something was missing. Maybe it came from having too much. Perhaps the jaw was oversized. Whatever the case, it was deceptive. Beauty Smith was widely recognized as the most spineless and whimpering of cowards. To round out his appearance, his teeth were big and yellowed, while his two canine teeth, larger than the rest, protruded beneath his thin lips like fangs. His eyes were yellow and cloudy, as if Nature had run out of pigments and mixed together the leftover remnants from all her paint tubes. The same applied to his hair, which grew sparsely and unevenly, muddy-yellow and dirty-yellow in color, sticking up from his head and jutting out from his face in random clumps and patches, looking like tangled and windswept grain.

In short, Beauty Smith was a monstrosity, but he wasn't to blame for it. The responsibility lay elsewhere. He wasn't accountable for what he had become. The clay of his being had been shaped that way during his creation. He handled the cooking for the other men at the fort, along with washing dishes and performing menial tasks. The men didn't look down on him. Instead, they put up with him in a broadly human way, the same way people tolerate any creature that has been badly treated during its formation. They also feared him. His cowardly fits of rage made them worry about getting shot in the back or finding poison in their coffee. But someone had to handle the cooking, and despite all his other flaws, Beauty Smith knew how to cook.

This was the man who watched White Fang, took pleasure in his savage abilities, and wanted to own him. From the beginning, he tried to win White Fang over. At first, White Fang simply ignored him. Later, when these attempts became more persistent,

White Fang raised his hackles, showed his teeth, and retreated. He disliked the man. Something about him felt wrong. He could sense the wickedness within him and was afraid of his outstretched hand and his attempts at gentle words. Because of all this, he despised the man.

With simpler creatures, good and bad are easily understood concepts. Good represents everything that brings comfort, satisfaction, and relief from pain. That's why good things are naturally liked. Bad represents everything filled with discomfort, threat, and harm, and is naturally hated. White Fang's impression of Beauty Smith was bad. From the man's deformed body and warped mind, in mysterious ways, like vapors rising from disease-ridden swamps, came signs of the sickness within him. Not through logical thinking, not through the five senses alone, but through other more distant and unknown senses, White Fang felt that this man was threatening with evil, filled with the potential to cause harm, and therefore something bad that should wisely be hated.

White Fang was in Grey Beaver's camp when Beauty Smith first came to visit. At the soft sound of footsteps in the distance, before the man even appeared, White Fang knew who was approaching and his fur began to stand on end. He had been lying down completely relaxed and comfortable, but he quickly got to his feet, and when the man arrived, he slipped away like a true wolf to the edge of the camp. He couldn't understand what they were saying, but he could watch the man and Grey Beaver talking together. At one point, the man pointed at him, and White Fang growled back as if that hand were about to come down on him instead of being fifty feet away as it actually was. The man laughed at this reaction, and White Fang crept away to the safety of the woods, keeping his head turned to watch as he moved silently across the ground.

Grey Beaver refused to sell the dog. His trading business had made him wealthy, and he didn't need anything. Moreover, White Fang was an extremely valuable animal—the most powerful sled dog he had ever owned and the finest leader he'd ever had. Additionally, there wasn't another dog like him anywhere along the Mackenzie or Yukon rivers. He was an exceptional fighter. He killed other dogs as effortlessly as people swat mosquitoes. (Beauty Smith's eyes gleamed when he heard this, and he ran his eager tongue across his thin lips). No, White Fang wasn't for sale at any price.

But Beauty Smith understood how to deal with Indians. He frequently visited Grey Beaver's camp, and he always carried one or more black bottles concealed beneath his coat. One of whisky's powerful effects is that it creates an insatiable craving. Grey Beaver developed this craving. His inflamed throat and burning stomach started demanding more and more of the fiery liquid, while his mind, completely disrupted by the unfamiliar stimulant, allowed him to do anything necessary to get it. The money he had earned from selling his furs, mittens, and moccasins started disappearing. It vanished more and more quickly, and as his money pouch grew lighter, his temper grew shorter.

In the end, his money, possessions, and self-control were completely depleted. All that remained was his overwhelming craving for alcohol, a massive burden that became even more intense with each moment of sobriety. It was then that Beauty Smith approached him once more to discuss purchasing White Fang, but this time the payment he offered came in bottles of liquor rather than cash, and Grey Beaver was far more interested in listening to this proposal.

"You catch the dog, you take it, all right," were his final words.

The bottles were delivered, but it took two days. "You catch the dog," Beauty Smith said to Grey Beaver.

White Fang crept into camp one evening and settled down with a contented sigh. The feared white god wasn't there. For days, his attempts to get his hands on him had become increasingly persistent, and during that time White Fang had been forced to stay away from the camp. He didn't understand what danger those persistent hands represented. He only knew that they meant some kind of harm, and that it was better for him to stay beyond their reach.

But he had barely settled down when Grey Beaver stumbled over to him and fastened a leather cord around his neck. He sat down next to White Fang, gripping the end of the cord in his hand. In his other hand he clutched a bottle, which he occasionally tilted above his head while making gurgling sounds.

An hour went by like this, when the vibrations of footsteps on the ground announced someone approaching. White Fang heard it first, and his fur was standing on end with recognition while Grey Beaver still sat nodding drowsily. White Fang tried to gently pull the rope from his master's hand; but the loose fingers gripped tightly and Grey Beaver woke up.

Beauty Smith walked into the camp and positioned himself above White Fang. White Fang growled quietly at this frightening figure, carefully watching every movement of the man's hands. One hand reached out and started moving down toward his head. His quiet growl became tight and rough. The hand kept slowly coming down while he crouched underneath it, staring at it with hatred, his growl becoming shorter and more intense as his breathing quickened and the hand drew closer to its target. All at once he struck, biting with his teeth like a snake. The hand pulled back quickly, and his teeth snapped together on nothing but air with a sharp clicking sound. Beauty Smith felt both scared and furious. Grey Beaver hit White Fang on the side of his head, making him crouch low against the ground in respectful submission.

White Fang watched with wary eyes, tracking every movement around him. He observed Beauty Smith leave and come back carrying a heavy club. Grey Beaver then handed the rope's end to Beauty Smith, who began walking away. The rope pulled tight as White Fang fought against it. Grey Beaver struck him from both sides, forcing him to stand and follow along. White Fang complied, but suddenly lunged forward, throwing himself at the stranger who was pulling him away. Beauty Smith didn't flinch or step back— he had anticipated this reaction. He swung the club with precision, halting White Fang's attack mid-charge and knocking him to the ground. Grey Beaver chuckled and showed his approval with a nod. Beauty Smith pulled the rope tight once more, and White Fang struggled weakly and unsteadily back to his feet.

He didn't charge again. A single blow from the club was enough to show him that the white god knew how to use it, and he was too smart to fight what couldn't be changed. So he trudged along behind Beauty Smith with his tail tucked between his legs, growling quietly under his breath. But Beauty Smith watched him carefully, keeping the club ready to strike at any moment.

At the fort, Beauty Smith secured him with tight bindings and went inside to sleep. White Fang waited for an hour. Then he used his teeth on the leather strap, and within ten seconds he was free. He hadn't wasted any time with his teeth. There was no pointless chewing. The strap was sliced through diagonally, almost as cleanly as if it had been cut with a knife. White Fang gazed up at the fort, his fur standing on end as he growled. Then he turned around and trotted back to Grey Beaver's camp. He felt no loyalty to this strange and frightening master. He had devoted himself to Grey Beaver, and he believed he still belonged to Grey Beaver.

But what had happened before happened again—with one important difference. Grey Beaver once more tied him up with a leather strap, and when morning came, he handed him over to Beauty Smith. This is where things changed. Beauty Smith gave him a brutal beating. Bound tightly, White Fang could only snarl helplessly and suffer through the punishment. Both club and whip were used on him, and he endured the most severe beating of his entire life. Even the harsh beating Grey Beaver had given him as a puppy seemed gentle compared to this one.

Beauty Smith took pleasure in the task. He reveled in it. He gloated over his victim, and his eyes burned with a dull flame as he wielded the whip or club and listened to White Fang's cries of pain and his helpless roars and snarls. Beauty Smith was cruel in the manner that cowards display cruelty. Cowering and whimpering when faced with the blows or harsh words of another man, he took his revenge, in return, on creatures weaker than himself. All living things crave power, and Beauty Smith was no different. Prevented from expressing power among his own species, he turned to lesser creatures and there justified the life force within him. However, Beauty Smith had not shaped himself, and no fault could be placed upon him. He had entered the world with a deformed body and a brutish mind. This had formed the raw material of his being, and the world had not molded it with kindness.

White Fang understood why he was receiving this beating. When Grey Beaver wrapped the leather strap around his neck and handed the other end to Beauty Smith, White Fang realized it was his master's decision for him to go with Beauty Smith. And when Beauty Smith left him tied up outside the fort, he understood that Beauty Smith wanted him to stay put. So he had gone against the wishes of both masters and deserved the punishment that followed. He had watched other dogs get new owners before, and he had seen runaway dogs get beaten just like he was being beaten now. He was intelligent, but there were instincts within him that were stronger than intelligence. Loyalty was one of these forces. He didn't feel love for Grey Beaver, but even when facing his master's decision and rage, he remained devoted to him. He couldn't control this feeling. This devotion was built into his very nature. It was a trait that belonged specifically to his kind; the characteristic that distinguished his species from every other species; the quality that allowed wolves and wild dogs to leave the wilderness

After the beating, White Fang was dragged back to the fort. However, this time Beauty Smith secured him with a stick. People don't abandon their gods easily, and the same was true for White Fang. Grey Beaver was his personal deity, and despite Grey Beaver's decision, White Fang continued to hold onto him and refused to let go. Grey Beaver had betrayed and abandoned him, but this didn't change anything for White Fang. He hadn't given himself completely to Grey Beaver for nothing. White Fang had held nothing back in his devotion, and such a deep connection couldn't be severed easily.

So, during the night, while the men in the fort slept, White Fang used his teeth on the stick that restrained him. The wood was aged and dry, and it was fastened so tightly to his neck that he could barely reach it with his teeth. Only through extreme physical effort and arching his neck was he able to get the wood between his teeth, and just barely at that; and only through tremendous patience, lasting many hours, did he manage to gnaw through the stick. This was something dogs weren't expected to do. It had never happened before. But White Fang accomplished it, running away from the fort in the early morning with the broken end of the stick still attached to his neck.

He was intelligent. However, if he had only been intelligent, he wouldn't have returned to Grey Beaver, who had already betrayed him twice before. Yet his loyalty compelled him, and he went back only to face betrayal for a third time. Once more he submitted to Grey Beaver fastening a rope around his neck, and once again Beauty Smith arrived to take possession of him. This time the beating he received was even more brutal than what he had endured previously.

Grey Beaver watched without emotion as the white man used the whip. He offered no protection. The dog was no longer his. After the beating ended, White Fang was severely injured. A pampered southern dog would have died from such treatment, but he survived. His harsh upbringing had toughened him, and he was made of stronger material. He possessed too much life force. His grip on survival was too powerful. However, he was badly hurt. Initially, he couldn't move himself forward, and Beauty Smith had to wait thirty minutes for him to recover. Then, unable to see clearly and stumbling, he trailed behind Beauty Smith as they returned to the fort.

But now he was bound by a chain that his teeth couldn't break, and he struggled uselessly, throwing himself forward to try to pull the metal fastener from the wood where it had been hammered in. After several days, sober and broke, Grey Beaver left up the Porcupine River on his long trip to the Mackenzie. White Fang stayed behind on the Yukon, now owned by a man who was more than half insane and completely savage. But how could a dog understand madness in his mind? To White Fang, Beauty Smith was a real, though frightening, god. He might have been a crazy god, but White Fang understood nothing about insanity; he only knew that he had to give in to this new master's will, follow his every desire and impulse.

Chapter III: The Reign of Hate

Under the guidance of the insane god, White Fang transformed into a demon. He was kept chained in a cage at the back of the fort, and there Beauty Smith tormented and provoked him, driving him to madness with constant small cruelties. The man quickly learned that White Fang was particularly sensitive to laughter, and he made sure to laugh at him after each painful trick he played. This laughter was loud and mocking, and at the same time the god would point his finger mockingly at White Fang. During these moments, all rational thought abandoned White Fang, and in his fits of fury he became even more crazed than Beauty Smith himself.

In the past, White Fang had simply been an enemy to other wolves and dogs, though certainly a fierce one. Now he became hostile toward everything that existed, and with greater savagery than before. The torment he endured was so severe that his hatred became blind and completely unreasonable. He despised the chain that restrained him, the people who stared at him through the gaps in his cage, the dogs that came with those people and growled viciously at him while he remained powerless. He even hated the actual wooden boards of the enclosure that trapped him. But above everything else, from beginning to end, he hated Beauty Smith most of all.

But Beauty Smith had a purpose behind everything he did to White Fang. One day several men gathered around the pen. Beauty Smith went inside, carrying a club, and removed the chain from White Fang's neck. After his master left, White Fang broke free and raced around the enclosure, desperately trying to reach the men standing outside. He looked magnificently terrifying. Measuring a full five feet in length and standing two and a half feet tall at the shoulder, he was much heavier than a wolf of similar size. He had inherited the bulkier build of a dog from his mother, which meant he weighed over ninety pounds despite having no fat and not an ounce of unnecessary flesh. His body was pure muscle, bone, and sinew—fighting flesh in perfect condition.

The pen door was opening once more. White Fang stopped and waited. Something out of the ordinary was taking place. He remained still, watching. The door swung open wider. Then an enormous dog was shoved inside, and the door slammed shut behind the animal. White Fang had never encountered such a dog before (it was a mastiff); however, the newcomer's massive size and threatening appearance didn't intimidate him. Here was something alive, neither wood nor metal, on which he could unleash his fury. He sprang forward in a blur of teeth that tore along the mastiff's neck. The mastiff shook his head, let out a deep growl, and lunged at White Fang. But White Fang moved like lightning, appearing here and there and everywhere, constantly dodging and avoiding contact, while repeatedly darting in to strike with his fangs before leaping back out of reach to avoid retaliation.

The men outside yelled and cheered, while Beauty Smith, overwhelmed with joy, reveled in the tearing and mauling that White Fang delivered. From the beginning, there was no chance for the mastiff to win. The dog was too heavy and sluggish. Finally, as Beauty Smith drove White Fang back using a club, the mastiff's owner pulled his dog away. Afterward, bets were settled, and coins jingled in Beauty Smith's palm.

White Fang began to anticipate with excitement the moments when men would gather around his enclosure. It signaled a fight was coming, and this had become his only outlet for expressing the vitality that burned within him. Tormented and provoked into hatred, he remained trapped as a prisoner with no means of releasing that rage except when his master decided to pit another dog against him. Beauty Smith had accurately assessed his capabilities, as White Fang consistently emerged victorious. On one occasion, three dogs were released into his pen one after another. Another time, a fully grown wolf, recently captured from the wilderness, was pushed through the pen's entrance. On yet another day, two dogs were set upon him simultaneously. This proved to be his most brutal battle, and although he ultimately killed both opponents, he was nearly killed himself in the process.

In the fall of that year, as the first snowflakes began to fall and slush ice started flowing down the river, Beauty Smith bought passage for himself and White Fang on a steamboat heading up the Yukon River to Dawson. White Fang had by now earned quite a reputation throughout the territory. Known far and wide as "the Fighting Wolf," the cage where he was confined on the steamboat's deck was constantly surrounded by curious onlookers. He would rage and growl at them, or sometimes lie still and observe them with cold, burning hatred. Why shouldn't he despise them? He never bothered to ask himself this question. He understood only hatred and lost himself completely in its intensity. His existence had transformed into pure torment. He hadn't been created to endure the tight captivity that wild animals suffer under human control. Yet this was exactly how he found himself being treated. People would gawk at him, thrust sticks through the bars to provoke his snarling, and then mock him with their laughter.

These men formed his world, and they were shaping him into something far more savage than Nature had ever planned. Yet Nature had blessed him with adaptability. While countless other animals would have perished or been completely broken in spirit, he found ways to survive and thrive without sacrificing his inner strength. Perhaps Beauty Smith, that master of cruelty and torment, possessed the ability to crush White Fang's spirit, but so far there was no indication he was getting close to success.

If Beauty Smith carried a devil within him, White Fang possessed one as well; and these two demons battled against each other without end. In earlier times, White Fang had possessed the sense to crouch low and surrender to a man wielding a club; but this intelligence had now abandoned him. Simply seeing Beauty Smith was enough to throw him into fits of rage. And when they engaged in close combat, and he had been driven back by the club, he continued growling and snarling, baring his teeth. The final growl could never be forced out of him. No matter how brutally he was beaten, he always had another growl ready; and when Beauty Smith finally gave up and retreated, the rebellious growl pursued him, or White Fang lunged at the cage bars roaring his hatred.

When the steamboat reached Dawson, White Fang stepped onto the shore. However, he continued to live his life in public view, confined within a cage and surrounded by curious onlookers. He was put on display as "the Fighting Wolf," with spectators paying fifty cents in gold dust for the chance to see him. He received no opportunity to rest. Whenever he lay down to sleep, someone would prod him with a sharp stick to ensure the audience received their money's worth. To make the show more captivating, his handlers kept him in a constant state of anger. Yet what proved even worse than all of this was the environment he was forced to endure. People viewed him as the most terrifying of wild creatures, and this perception reached him through the bars of his enclosure. Every spoken word and every careful movement from the men reinforced his own savage nature. This treatment served as additional fuel for the fire of his wildness. Only one outcome was possible: his ferocity began feeding on itself and growing stronger. This represented yet another example of how adaptable his nature was, demonstrating his ability to be shaped by the forces of his surroundings.

In addition to being put on display, he was a professional fighting animal. At unpredictable times, whenever a fight could be set up, he was removed from his cage and taken into the woods several miles outside of town. This usually happened at night to avoid interference from the Territory's mounted police. After waiting for a few hours until daylight came, the audience and the dog he was supposed to fight would show up. This is how he ended up fighting dogs of all different sizes and breeds. It was a brutal land, the men were brutal, and the fights typically ended in death.

Since White Fang kept fighting, it's clear that the other dogs were the ones who died. He never experienced defeat. His early training, when he battled with Lip-lip and the entire puppy pack, served him well. There was the determination with which he held his ground. No dog could make him lose his balance. This was the preferred strategy of the wolf breeds—to charge at him, either straight on or with a sudden change of direction, hoping to hit his shoulder and knock him down. Mackenzie hounds, Eskimo and Labrador dogs, huskies and Malemutes—all attempted this move on him, and all were unsuccessful. He was never known to lose his balance. Men shared this fact with each other, and watched each time expecting it to happen; but White Fang always let them down.

Then there was his incredible speed. This gave him a huge advantage over his opponents. Regardless of their fighting background, they had never faced a dog that could move as fast as he could. Another factor to consider was how instantly he would strike. Most dogs were used to the usual warning signs of snarling, bristling, and growling, but the typical dog would be knocked down and defeated before it had even started fighting or gotten over its shock. This happened so frequently that it became standard practice to restrain White Fang until the other dog completed its threatening displays, was fully prepared, and had even launched the first attack.

White Fang's greatest advantage, however, was his experience. He understood fighting better than any dog he faced. He had been in more battles, knew how to counter more tactics and techniques, and possessed more strategies of his own, while his personal fighting style was nearly perfect.

As time passed, he fought less and less frequently. Men gave up hope of finding anyone who could match him, and Beauty Smith was forced to make him fight wolves instead. The Indians trapped these wolves specifically for this purpose, and a battle between White Fang and a wolf never failed to attract a crowd. On one occasion, they captured a fully grown female lynx, and this time White Fang was fighting for his very survival. Her speed was equal to his; her savagery matched his own; while he could only fight with his teeth, she fought with her razor-sharp claws as well.

But after the lynx, all fighting stopped for White Fang. There were no more animals left to fight—at least, none that were considered worthy opponents for him. So he stayed on display until spring arrived, when a man named Tim Keenan, who dealt faro cards for a living, came to the territory. He brought with him the first bulldog that had ever set foot in the Klondike. It was inevitable that this dog and White Fang would eventually face each other, and for an entire week the upcoming fight became the main topic of conversation in certain parts of town.

Chapter IV: The Clinging Death

Beauty Smith removed the chain from his neck and took a step backward.

For once White Fang didn't launch into an immediate attack. He remained motionless, ears standing upright, alert and curious as he studied the unusual animal confronting him. He had never encountered such a dog before. Tim Keenan pushed the bulldog forward with a mumbled "Go to it." The creature waddled toward the center of the circle, short and stocky and awkward. It came to a halt and blinked across at White Fang.

There were shouts from the crowd: "Go get him, Cherokee! Attack him, Cherokee! Tear him apart!"

But Cherokee didn't appear eager to fight. He turned his head and blinked at the shouting men while wagging his stubby tail in a friendly manner. He wasn't scared, just lazy. Moreover, he didn't think he was supposed to fight the dog standing in front of him. He wasn't accustomed to fighting that type of dog and was waiting for them to bring out the actual opponent.

Tim Keenan stepped forward and leaned over Cherokee, stroking him on both sides of his shoulders with hands that moved against the direction of his fur and made small, forward-pushing motions. These actions served as deliberate provocations. Their effect was clearly agitating, as Cherokee started to growl quietly, deep in his throat. There was a perfect synchronization between the growling and the man's hand movements. The growl would build in Cherokee's throat as each forward-pushing motion reached its peak, then fade away only to begin again with the start of the next movement. Each motion ended with a sharp emphasis in the rhythm, the movement stopping suddenly while the growling surged upward with an abrupt intensity.

This had a clear impact on White Fang. The fur on his neck and shoulders started to stand up. Tim Keenan gave one last push forward and stepped back. As the momentum that propelled Cherokee forward faded, he kept moving ahead on his own, running in a quick, bow-legged stride. Then White Fang attacked. A shout of surprised amazement erupted from the crowd. He had closed the gap and struck more like a cat than a dog, and with that same feline speed, he had slashed with his teeth and jumped away to safety.

The bulldog was bleeding behind one ear from a tear in his thick neck. He showed no reaction, didn't even growl, but turned and continued pursuing White Fang. The performance from both animals—the speed of one and the persistence of the other—had stirred up the competitive spirit of the crowd, and the men were placing new bets and raising their existing wagers. Once more, and then again, White Fang lunged forward, struck, and escaped unharmed, while his unusual opponent kept following him, neither rushing nor moving slowly, but with deliberate determination in a methodical manner. There was clear intention behind his approach—he had something specific to accomplish that he was focused on completing, and nothing could divert his attention from it.

His entire behavior and every movement reflected this single-minded determination. This baffled White Fang completely. He had never encountered a dog like this before. The creature had no protective fur covering. Its skin was tender and wounded easily. Unlike the dogs from his own species that often frustrated his attacks with their thick, matted coats, this animal offered no such resistance. Every time White Fang's teeth made contact, they penetrated effortlessly into the soft flesh, and the creature seemed incapable of protecting itself. What made the situation even more unsettling was the animal's silence—it didn't cry out like the other dogs White Fang had battled in the past. Apart from an occasional growl or grunt, the dog endured its injuries without making a sound. And despite everything, it never gave up chasing him.

Cherokee wasn't slow by any means. He could pivot and spin quickly enough, but White Fang was never in the same spot. Cherokee felt confused as well. He had never before battled a dog that wouldn't engage in close combat. The urge to grapple had always been shared by both fighters. Yet here stood an opponent that maintained its distance, weaving and evading in every direction. And whenever it managed to sink its teeth into him, it wouldn't maintain its grip but released immediately and sprang away once more.

White Fang couldn't reach the vulnerable soft flesh of the throat. The bulldog was too low to the ground, and its powerful jaws provided extra defense. White Fang darted in and out without injury, while Cherokee's wounds kept getting worse. Both sides of his neck and head were torn and cut open. He bled heavily, but showed no signs of being troubled. He kept up his steady pursuit, though once, momentarily confused, he stopped completely and looked at the watching men, wagging his stubby tail at the same time to show he was ready to keep fighting.

In that instant, White Fang struck and retreated, tearing at what remained of Cherokee's cropped ear as he passed. Showing just a hint of irritation, Cherokee resumed the chase, running along the inner edge of the circle White Fang was creating while trying to lock his lethal bite onto White Fang's throat. The bulldog came within a fraction of an inch of success, and shouts of admiration erupted as White Fang suddenly spun away from danger in the other direction.

Time passed. White Fang continued his dance, dodging and weaving, darting in and out, constantly inflicting wounds. Meanwhile, the bulldog pursued him with grim determination. Eventually he would achieve his goal, securing the grip that would decide the fight. For now, he endured whatever punishment his opponent could deliver. His ear tufts had been torn into ragged strips, his neck and shoulders bore cuts in dozens of places, and even his lips were sliced and bleeding—all from those lightning-fast strikes that he couldn't anticipate or defend against.

Time and again White Fang had tried to knock Cherokee off his feet, but the difference in their height was too great. Cherokee was too low to the ground, too compact. White Fang attempted the maneuver once too many times. The opportunity presented itself during one of his rapid direction changes and circular movements. He caught Cherokee with his head turned away as the dog spun around more slowly. Cherokee's shoulder was left unprotected. White Fang lunged at it, but his own shoulder was positioned much higher, and he struck with such tremendous force that his forward momentum sent him tumbling over his opponent's body. For the first time in all his battles, spectators witnessed White Fang lose his balance. His body flipped halfway through the air, and he would have crashed onto his back if he hadn't twisted like a cat while still airborne, struggling to get his feet beneath him. Even so, he hit the ground hard on his side. The next moment he was back on his feet, but in that brief instant

Cherokee's teeth had clamped down on his throat.

It wasn't a good grip, positioned too low near the chest, but Cherokee held on tight. White Fang jumped to his feet and thrashed around wildly, desperately trying to shake off the bulldog's weight. This clinging, dragging burden drove him into a frenzy. It restricted his movements and limited his freedom. The sensation reminded him of being trapped, and every instinct within him fought against it with fierce resistance. His revolt was absolutely wild. For several minutes, he seemed completely out of his mind. The fundamental life force within him took complete control. His body's desperate will to survive overwhelmed everything else. He became consumed by nothing but the raw, physical love of life itself. All rational thought disappeared entirely. It was as if his brain had simply stopped working. His ability to reason was completely overthrown by the flesh's blind, desperate need to exist and keep moving—to move at any cost, to never stop moving, because movement itself was the very expression of being alive.

Round and round he spun, whirling and twisting and changing direction, attempting to throw off the fifty-pound burden that pulled at his throat. The bulldog did nothing except maintain his hold. Occasionally, though not often, he succeeded in getting his paws on the ground and briefly steadying himself against White Fang. But the following instant his balance would be gone and he would be pulled around in the spiral of one of White Fang's frenzied spins. Cherokee became one with his instinct. He understood that he was acting correctly by hanging on, and waves of joyful satisfaction washed over him. During these moments he actually shut his eyes and let his body be thrown back and forth, helplessly, unconcerned about any injury that might result. That was unimportant. The grip was everything, and the grip he maintained.

White Fang only stopped when he had completely exhausted himself. He was powerless, and he couldn't comprehend what was happening. In all his battles, nothing like this had ever occurred. The dogs he had previously fought didn't use these tactics. Their approach was always to bite and claw and retreat, bite and claw and retreat. He lay partially on his side, gasping for air. Cherokee maintained his hold, pressing against him, attempting to force him completely onto his side. White Fang fought back, and he could sense the jaws adjusting their position, loosening slightly before clamping down again in a grinding motion. Each adjustment brought the grip nearer to his throat. The bulldog's strategy was to secure what he had captured, and when the moment was right, to work toward gaining more. The moment was right when White Fang stayed still. When White Fang fought back, Cherokee was satisfied simply to maintain his hold.

The thick, bulging back of Cherokee's neck was the only part of his body that White Fang's teeth could reach. He managed to get a grip near the base where the neck emerged from the shoulders, but he didn't understand the grinding method of combat, and his jaws weren't built for it. He frantically ripped and tore with his fangs for a moment. Then a shift in their position distracted him. The bulldog had succeeded in rolling him onto his back, and while still gripping his throat, was now on top of him. Like a cat, White Fang drew his hindquarters up, and with his feet digging into his enemy's belly above him, he started clawing with long, raking strokes. Cherokee could easily have been gutted if he hadn't quickly twisted on his hold and moved his body off White Fang's and positioned it at a right angle to him.

There was no escaping that grip. It was like Fate itself, and just as relentless. Gradually it moved up along the throat. All that prevented White Fang from dying was the loose skin of his neck and the dense fur that covered it. This created a large fold in Cherokee's mouth, the fur of which nearly resisted his teeth. But little by little, whenever the opportunity arose, he was getting more of the loose skin and fur in his mouth. The consequence was that he was gradually choking White Fang. White Fang's breathing became more and more labored as time passed.

It started to seem like the fight was finished. Cherokee's supporters became excited and confident, offering absurd betting odds. White Fang's supporters felt equally discouraged and turned down bets of ten to one and twenty to one, although one person was foolish enough to accept a wager of fifty to one. This person was Beauty Smith. He stepped forward into the ring and pointed his finger directly at White Fang. Then he started laughing mockingly and with contempt. This achieved exactly what he wanted. White Fang became furious with rage. He summoned his remaining strength and managed to get back on his feet. As he moved around the ring, with the fifty pounds of his opponent constantly pulling at his throat, his fury transformed into terror. His basic survival instincts took control of him once more, and his reasoning disappeared as his body's desperate need to survive took over. Around and around and back again, stumbling and falling and getting up, sometimes even standing on his back legs and lifting his enemy completely off the ground, he fought desperately but unsuccessfully to free himself from this deadly grip.

Finally, White Fang collapsed, falling backward in complete exhaustion; the bulldog immediately adjusted his hold, moving in closer, tearing apart more and more of the fur-covered flesh, choking White Fang more brutally than before. Cheers erupted for the winner, and numerous voices shouted "Cherokee!" "Cherokee!" Cherokee responded to this by enthusiastically wagging what remained of his tail. However, the roar of approval didn't break his concentration. There was no connection between his tail and his powerful jaws. His tail might wag, but his jaws maintained their deadly grip on White Fang's throat.

It was at this moment that the spectators received an unexpected distraction. The sound of jingling bells filled the air. The shouts of dog sledders could be heard in the distance. Everyone except Beauty Smith glanced around nervously, their fear of the police weighing heavily on their minds. However, they noticed two men approaching from up the trail rather than down, running alongside their sled and dogs. They were clearly returning from a prospecting expedition somewhere up the creek. When they spotted the gathered crowd, they brought their dogs to a halt and walked over to join the group, eager to discover what was causing all the commotion. One of the dog sledders sported a mustache, while his companion, who was taller and younger, had a clean-shaven face with skin that glowed pink from his vigorous circulation and their run through the crisp, cold air.

White Fang had almost completely stopped fighting back. Every so often he would struggle frantically but without any real effect. He could barely breathe, and what little air he managed to get grew smaller and smaller as the relentless grip continued to tighten around him. Despite the thick protection of his fur coat, the major blood vessel in his throat would have been ripped apart long ago if the bulldog's initial bite hadn't been positioned so low that it was essentially on his chest. It had taken Cherokee considerable time to work that grip higher up, and this had also caused his jaws to become increasingly clogged with fur and folds of skin.

Meanwhile, the savage beast within Beauty Smith had been climbing into his mind and taking control of what little sanity he had to begin with. When he saw White Fang's eyes starting to grow dim, he knew without question that the fight was over. That's when he lost control completely. He lunged at White Fang and began brutally kicking him. The crowd hissed and shouted in protest, but that was all they did. While this was happening, and Beauty Smith kept kicking White Fang, there was a disturbance in the crowd. The tall young stranger was pushing his way through, shoving men aside left and right without any politeness or care. When he burst through into the ring, Beauty Smith was just about to deliver another kick. All his weight rested on one foot, and he was completely off balance. At that exact moment, the newcomer's fist connected with a crushing blow right to his face. Beauty Smith's other leg came off the ground, and his entire body seemed to fly through the air as he flipped backward and hit the snow. The newcomer then turned to face the crowd.

"You cowards!" he shouted. "You animals!"

He was furious himself—a controlled fury. His gray eyes looked metallic and steel-like as they blazed at the crowd. Beauty Smith got back on his feet and approached him, sniveling and acting like a coward. The newcomer didn't understand what was happening. He didn't realize what a pathetic coward the other man was, and assumed he was coming back to continue the fight. So, shouting "You beast!" he knocked Beauty Smith backward with another punch to the face. Beauty Smith decided that staying down in the snow was the safest option for him, and remained where he had fallen, making no attempt to stand up.

"Come on, Matt, give me a hand," the newcomer called to the dog-musher, who had followed him into the ring.

Both men leaned down over the dogs. Matt grabbed hold of White Fang, prepared to pull him away as soon as Cherokee's jaws could be pried open. The younger man tried to make this happen by gripping the bulldog's jaws with his hands and attempting to force them apart. It was a hopeless effort. As he pulled and yanked and twisted, he kept shouting with each labored breath, "Beasts!"

The crowd started becoming restless, and several men began complaining about ruining their entertainment; however, they fell silent when the stranger raised his head from what he was doing for a moment and stared at them menacingly.

"You damn beasts!" he finally exploded, and went back to his task.

"It's no use, Mr. Scott, you can't break them apart that way," Matt said at last.

The two stopped and looked at the chained dogs.

"It's not bleeding much," Matt announced. "It hasn't gone all the way in yet."

"But he could lose his hold at any second," Scott replied. "There, did you see that! He adjusted his grip slightly."

The young man's excitement and fear for White Fang kept building. He hit Cherokee in the head brutally over and over again. But this didn't make the jaws let go. Cherokee wagged what remained of his tail to show that he understood what the blows meant, but that he knew he was right and was simply doing what he was supposed to do by maintaining his grip.

"Won't some of you help?" Scott shouted desperately to the crowd.

But no one offered to help. Instead, the crowd started sarcastically cheering him on and bombarded him with mocking advice.

"You'll need to get a crowbar," Matt advised.

The other man reached into the holster on his hip, pulled out his revolver, and attempted to force its barrel between the bulldog's jaws. He pushed and pushed forcefully until the scraping sound of steel against clenched teeth could be clearly heard. Both men were kneeling, leaning over the dogs. Tim Keenan walked into the ring. He stopped next to Scott and placed his hand on his shoulder, speaking in a threatening tone:

"Don't break those teeth, stranger."

"Then I'll break his neck," Scott shot back, continuing to push and jam with the gun barrel.

"I told you not to break those teeth," the faro dealer said again, his voice more threatening than before.

But if he was trying to bluff, it didn't work. Scott never stopped his efforts, though he looked up calmly and asked:

"Your dog?"

The faro dealer grunted.

"Then get in here and break this grip."

"Well, stranger," the other said in an irritatingly slow manner, "I don't mind telling you that's something I haven't figured out for myself. I don't know how to pull it off."

"Then get out of the way," was the reply, "and don't bother me. I'm busy."

Tim Keenan remained standing above him, but Scott paid no attention to his presence. He had succeeded in wedging the muzzle between the jaws on one side and was attempting to work it out between the jaws on the other side. Once he achieved this, he pried slowly and cautiously, gradually loosening the jaws little by little, while Matt, bit by bit, freed White Fang's torn neck.

"Get ready to take back your dog," Scott commanded Cherokee's owner firmly.

The faro dealer bent down as instructed and grabbed Cherokee securely.

"Now!" Scott warned, giving the final push with the crowbar.

The dogs were pulled apart, with the bulldog fighting hard to break free.

"Take him away," Scott ordered, and Tim Keenan pulled Cherokee back into the crowd.

White Fang tried several times to stand up, but each attempt failed. He managed to get to his feet once, but his legs were too weak to hold him, and he gradually collapsed back into the snow. His eyes were barely open, with a glassy look covering their surface. His mouth hung open, and his tongue stuck out, wet and lifeless. He looked exactly like a dog that had been choked to death. Matt looked him over.

"He's almost completely exhausted," he announced, "but his breathing is normal."

Beauty Smith got back on his feet and walked over to take a look at White Fang.

"Matt, what's the value of a quality sled dog?" Scott asked.

The dog-sled driver, still kneeling and bent over White Fang, thought for a moment.

"Three hundred dollars," he answered.

"And what's the price for one that's all beaten up like this?" Scott asked, giving White Fang a gentle push with his foot.

"Half of that," the dog-musher declared. Scott turned to face Beauty Smith.

"Did you hear, Mr. Beast? I'm going to take your dog from you, and I'm going to give you a hundred and fifty for him."

He opened his wallet and counted out the money.

Beauty Smith placed his hands behind his back, refusing to touch the money being offered to him.

"I'm not selling," he said.

"Oh, yes you are," the other assured him. "Because I'm buying. Here's your money. The dog's mine."

Beauty Smith, with his hands still behind him, started to back away.

Scott lunged forward, pulling his fist back to throw a punch. Beauty Smith crouched down, bracing himself for the hit.

"I have my rights," he whimpered.

"You've given up your right to own that dog," came the response. "Are you going to take the money? Or do I need to hit you again?"

"All right," Beauty Smith said quickly, his voice sharp with fear. "But I'm taking this money under protest," he added. "That dog is worth a fortune. I'm not going to let myself be robbed. A man has his rights."

"That's right," Scott replied, handing him the money. "A man has his rights. But you're not a man. You're an animal."

"Just wait until I return to Dawson," Beauty Smith threatened. "I'll bring the law down on you."

"If you say anything when you return to Dawson, I'll make sure you're forced to leave town. Do you understand?"

Beauty Smith responded with a grunt.

"Do you understand?" the other roared with sudden intensity.

"Yes," Beauty Smith grunted, pulling back.

"Yes what?"

"Yes, sir," Beauty Smith snarled.

"Watch out! He'll bite!" someone yelled, and a burst of laughter erupted.

Scott turned away from him and went back to help the dog driver, who was tending to White Fang.

Some of the men were already leaving; others stood around in small groups, watching and talking. Tim Keenan joined one of the groups.

"Who's that guy?" he asked.

"Weedon Scott," someone answered.

"And who the hell is Weedon Scott?" the faro dealer asked.

"Oh, he's one of those top-notch mining experts. He's connected with all the important people. If you want to stay out of trouble, you'll keep away from him, that's my advice. He's on good terms with the officials. The Gold Commissioner is a close friend of his."

"I figured he had to be someone important," the faro dealer remarked. "That's why I kept my hands off him from the beginning."

Chapter V: The Indomitable

"It's hopeless," Weedon Scott confessed.

He sat on the step of his cabin and stared at the dog-musher, who responded with a shrug that was equally hopeless.

Together they watched White Fang at the end of his taut chain, his fur standing on end, growling and snarling with fierce intensity as he strained to reach the sled dogs. After Matt had taught them several harsh lessons with his club, the sled dogs had learned to keep their distance from White Fang; even now they lay far away, seemingly ignoring his presence entirely.

"It's a wolf and there's no taming it," Weedon Scott declared.

"Oh, I'm not so sure about that," Matt disagreed. "There might be a lot of dog in him, for all we know. But there's one thing I'm certain of, and there's no escaping it."

The sled dog driver stopped and gave a knowing nod toward Moosehide Mountain.

"Well, don't be stingy with what you know," Scott said sharply, after waiting an appropriate amount of time. "Tell me. What is it?"

The dog-musher pointed to White Fang with a backward jerk of his thumb.

"Wolf or dog, it doesn't matter—he's already been tamed."

"No!"

"I'm telling you yes, and broken to harness. Look closely there. Do you see those marks across the chest?"

"You're right, Matt. He was a sled dog before Beauty Smith got hold of him."

"And there's not much reason against him being a sled dog again."

"What do you think?" Scott asked eagerly. Then the hope faded as he added, shaking his head, "We've had him for two weeks now, and if anything he's more wild than ever right now."

"Give him a chance," Matt advised. "Turn him loose for a while."

The other person stared at him in disbelief.

"Yes," Matt continued, "I know you've tried to, but you didn't take a club."

"You try it then."

The dog handler grabbed a club and walked over to the chained animal. White Fang watched the club like a caged lion watching its trainer's whip.

"Look at how he's watching that club," Matt said. "That's a good sign. He's not stupid. He won't dare attack me as long as I have this club within reach. He's definitely not completely insane."

As the man's hand moved toward his neck, White Fang bristled and snarled while crouching low. However, even as he watched the approaching hand, he managed to keep his eye on the club in the man's other hand, which hung menacingly above him. Matt unclipped the chain from the collar and stepped backward.

White Fang could barely believe that he was actually free. Many months had passed since Beauty Smith had taken ownership of him, and during that entire time he had never experienced even a single moment of freedom, except for those occasions when he was released to fight other dogs. Right after those fights, he was always locked up again.

He couldn't figure out what was happening. Maybe the gods were planning some new trick to play on him. He moved slowly and carefully, ready to be attacked at any second. He had no idea what to do since nothing like this had ever happened before. To be safe, he stayed away from the two gods who were watching him and walked cautiously to the corner of the cabin. Nothing occurred. He was clearly confused, so he returned, stopping about twelve feet away and staring intensely at the two men.

"Won't he run away?" his new owner asked.

Matt shrugged his shoulders. "We have to take a chance. The only way to discover the truth is to go ahead and see what happens."

"Poor guy," Scott whispered with sympathy. "What he needs is someone to show him a little human compassion," he said, turning around and walking into the cabin.

He emerged carrying a piece of meat, which he threw to White Fang. White Fang jumped back from it and examined it warily from a safe distance.

"Watch out, Major!" Matt yelled in warning, but it was too late.

Major lunged toward the meat. The moment his jaws clamped down on it, White Fang attacked him. Major was knocked down. Matt rushed forward, but White Fang was faster. Major struggled to get back on his feet, but blood gushing from his throat stained the snow in an expanding trail of red.

"It's unfortunate, but he got what he deserved," Scott said quickly.

But Matt's foot was already moving to kick White Fang. In an instant, there was a leap, a flash of teeth, and a sharp cry. White Fang, growling ferociously, scrambled backward several yards while Matt bent down to examine his leg.

"He got me good," he declared, gesturing toward his ripped pants and underwear, and the expanding patch of blood.

"I told you it was hopeless, Matt," Scott said in a discouraged voice. "I've been thinking about it on and off, even though I didn't want to. But we've reached that point now. It's the only option we have."

As he spoke, he reluctantly pulled out his revolver, opened the cylinder, and checked to make sure it was loaded.

"Listen here, Mr. Scott," Matt protested; "that dog has been through hell. You can't expect him to come out a white and shining angel. Give him time."

"Look at Major," the other replied.

The dog handler looked over the injured dog. The animal had

collapsed onto the snow in a pool of its own blood and was clearly taking its final breaths.

"He got what he deserved. You said it yourself, Mr. Scott. He tried to steal White Fang's food, and now he's dead. That's exactly what anyone should have expected. I wouldn't give a damn about a dog that won't fight to protect its own meal."

"But take a look at yourself, Matt. The dogs are one thing, but we have to draw the line somewhere."

"I deserved it," Matt insisted stubbornly. "Why did I want to kick him anyway? You said yourself that he had done the right thing. So I had no right to kick him."

"It would be a mercy to kill him," Scott insisted. "He can't be tamed."

"Listen here, Mr. Scott, give the poor guy a fighting chance. He hasn't had any opportunity yet. He's just been through hell, and this is the first time he's been free. Give him a fair chance, and if he doesn't deliver what's expected, I'll kill him myself. There!"

"God knows I don't want to kill him or have him killed," Scott replied, putting the revolver away. "We'll let him roam free and see what kindness can accomplish for him. And here's an attempt at it."

He walked over to White Fang and started speaking to him in a gentle and calming voice.

"You'd better keep a club within reach," Matt warned.

Scott shook his head and continued working to earn White Fang's trust.

White Fang felt wary. Something was about to happen. He had killed this god's dog, bitten his companion god, and what else could he expect except some terrible punishment? But facing this threat, he remained defiant. He bristled and bared his teeth, his eyes alert, his entire body cautious and ready for anything. The god carried no club, so he allowed him to come quite close. The god's hand had extended and was coming down toward his head. White

Fang pulled back and tensed as he crouched beneath it. Here was danger, some betrayal or something worse. He understood the hands of the gods, their proven dominance, their skill at inflicting pain. Moreover, there was his deep-rooted hatred of being touched. He growled more threateningly, crouched even lower, and still the hand came down. He didn't want to bite the hand, and he tolerated the danger of it until his instinct rose within him, overwhelming him with its relentless drive for survival.

Weedon Scott thought he was fast enough to dodge any bite or swipe. However, he still needed to discover White Fang's incredible speed, as White Fang attacked with the precision and quickness of a striking serpent.

Scott cried out in sharp surprise, grabbing his injured hand and gripping it tightly with his other hand. Matt let out a loud curse and rushed to his side. White Fang crouched low and retreated, his fur standing on end as he bared his teeth, his eyes filled with threatening malice. Now he could expect a beating as terrible as any he had endured from Beauty Smith.

"Hey! What are you doing?" Scott shouted suddenly.

Matt had rushed into the cabin and emerged with a rifle.

"Nothing," he said slowly, with a careless calmness that was put on, "just going to keep that promise I made. I figure it's up to me to kill him as I said I would do."

"No you don't!"

"Yes I do. Watch me."

As Matt had begged for White Fang's life when he had been bitten, it was now Weedon Scott's turn to beg.

"You told me to give him a chance. Well, let's give it to him. We've barely begun, and we can't give up right at the start. I got what I deserved this time. And—just look at him!"

White Fang stood near the corner of the cabin, about forty feet away, growling with terrifying ferocity—not at Scott, but at the dog handler.

"Well, I'll be completely amazed!" was the sled dog driver's expression of astonishment.

"Look how smart he is," Scott continued urgently. "He understands guns just as well as you do. He's intelligent and we need to give that intelligence a chance. Put the gun down."

"All right, I'm willing," Matt agreed, leaning the rifle against the woodpile.

"But will you look at that!" he exclaimed the next moment.

White Fang had calmed down and stopped snarling. "This is worth investigating. Watch."

Matt reached for the rifle, and at that exact moment White Fang growled menacingly. He moved away from the weapon, and White Fang's raised lips lowered back down, concealing his teeth.

"Now, just for fun."

Matt picked up the rifle and slowly began lifting it to his shoulder. As soon as he started moving, White Fang began snarling, and the growling grew louder as Matt continued raising the weapon. But just before the rifle could be aimed directly at him, White Fang jumped sideways and disappeared behind the corner of the cabin. Matt stood there, looking down the rifle's sights at the empty patch of snow where White Fang had been standing just moments before.

The dog-musher set down the rifle with gravity, then turned to face his employer.

"I agree with you, Mr. Scott. That dog is too intelligent to kill."

Chapter VI: The Love-Master

As White Fang watched Weedon Scott approach, his fur stood on end and he growled menacingly to make it clear that he wouldn't accept any punishment. Twenty-four hours had gone by since he had torn open the hand that was now wrapped in bandages and supported by a sling to prevent bleeding. White Fang had endured delayed punishments before, and he sensed that another one was coming his way. How could it be any different? He had done something that felt like a grave sin to him, burying his teeth into the sacred flesh of a god, and a white-skinned superior god no less. Given the natural order of things and his relationship with gods, something dreadful was waiting for him.

The god settled down a few feet away. White Fang couldn't see any threat in this position. When the gods delivered punishment, they remained standing on their feet. Moreover, this god carried no club, no whip, no weapon. And beyond that, he was completely free. No chain or stick restrained him. He could flee to safety while the god struggled to get back on his feet. For now, he would wait and observe what happened.

The god stayed silent and didn't move at all; White Fang's snarl gradually faded to a growl that died away in his throat and stopped completely. Then the god began to speak, and at the very first sound of his voice, the fur on White Fang's neck stood up and the growl surged back up his throat. But the god made no threatening gesture and continued speaking in a calm manner. For a while White Fang growled along with him, creating a matching rhythm between his growl and the man's voice. But the god kept talking without stopping. He spoke to White Fang in a way that White Fang had never experienced before. He spoke quietly and gently, with a kindness that somehow, in some way, reached White Fang. Despite himself and all the sharp warnings from his instincts, White Fang started to trust this god. He felt a sense of safety that went against everything he had learned from his encounters with humans.

After a considerable amount of time, the god stood up and walked into the cabin. White Fang watched him nervously when he emerged. He carried no whip, club, or weapon of any kind. His unharmed hand wasn't concealed behind his back, hiding anything threatening. He settled down in the exact same position as before, maintaining the same distance of several feet. He extended a small morsel of meat toward White Fang. White Fang's ears perked up as he examined it with deep suspicion, somehow managing to keep his gaze fixed on both the meat and the god simultaneously, staying vigilant for any aggressive movement, his muscles coiled and prepared to leap away at the slightest indication of danger.

The punishment still didn't come. The god simply held a piece of meat close to his nose. There appeared to be nothing wrong with the meat. Yet White Fang remained suspicious; even though the meat was offered to him with quick, encouraging movements of the hand, he wouldn't touch it. The gods possessed all wisdom, and there was no way to know what cunning deception might be hidden behind that seemingly innocent piece of meat. From previous experiences, particularly when dealing with squaws, meat and punishment had frequently been catastrophically connected.

In the end, the god threw the meat onto the snow at White Fang's feet. He sniffed the meat cautiously, but he didn't look at it. While he examined its scent, he kept his gaze fixed on the god. Nothing happened. He picked up the meat with his mouth and ate it. Still nothing occurred. The god was genuinely offering him another piece of meat. Once more he wouldn't take it directly from the hand, and once more it was thrown to him. This happened several times. But eventually there came a moment when the god refused to throw it. He held it in his hand and persistently offered it.

The meat was excellent, and White Fang felt ravenous. Slowly and with extreme caution, he moved closer to the outstretched hand. Finally, the moment arrived when he made the decision to take the meat directly from the hand. His gaze remained fixed on the god throughout, pushing his head forward while his ears lay flat against his skull and his fur bristled involuntarily along his neck. A quiet growl also vibrated in his throat, serving as a warning that he should not be taken lightly. He consumed the meat, and nothing occurred. One morsel at a time, he devoured all the meat, and still nothing happened. The expected punishment continued to be delayed.

He licked his lips and waited. The god continued speaking. There was kindness in his voice—something White Fang had never experienced before. And within him it stirred feelings he had never felt previously. He sensed a peculiar contentment, as if some hunger were being satisfied, as if some emptiness inside him were being filled. But then his instincts kicked in again along with the caution born from past experience. The gods were always cunning, and they had mysterious methods of achieving their goals.

Ah, he had known it! There it was now, the god's hand, clever in its ability to cause pain, reaching out toward him, coming down on his head. But the god continued speaking. His voice was gentle and calming. Despite the threatening hand, the voice created trust. And despite the reassuring voice, the hand created suspicion. White Fang was pulled apart by opposing emotions and urges. It felt as though he might shatter completely, so intense was the effort he was making, held together only by an unusual uncertainty as the opposing forces battled inside him for control.

He found a middle ground. He growled and bristled, flattening his ears against his head. Yet he didn't snap or bolt away. The hand came down toward him. Closer and closer it moved. It brushed against the tips of his raised fur. He cowered beneath it. The hand followed him down, pressing more firmly against his body. Trembling, nearly shaking, he somehow managed to keep himself from breaking apart. This hand that touched him and went against every instinct he had was pure agony. He couldn't erase in a single day all the cruelty that men had inflicted upon him. But this was what the god wanted, and he fought to give in.

The hand rose and fell again in a gentle, soothing motion. This pattern persisted, but each time the hand rose, the fur beneath it bristled upward. And each time the hand came down, his ears pressed flat against his head while a deep, rumbling growl rose from his throat. White Fang continued growling with persistent warning. Through this behavior he made it clear that he was ready to fight back against any harm that might come to him. There was no way to know when the god's hidden intentions might be revealed. At any instant that quiet, reassuring voice could explode into an angry roar, that tender and gentle hand could turn into an iron grip that would pin him down helplessly and deliver punishment.

But the god continued speaking in gentle tones, and his hand kept moving up and down in friendly pats. White Fang felt conflicted emotions. This went against his natural instincts. It held him back and worked against his desire for freedom. Yet it didn't cause him any physical pain. In fact, it actually felt good in a physical sense. The patting motion gradually and gently shifted to rubbing around the base of his ears, and the physical pleasure grew slightly stronger. Still, he remained afraid, staying alert and ready for some unknown danger, switching between discomfort and enjoyment as one feeling or the other took control of him.

"Well, I'll be completely amazed!"

Matt emerged from the cabin with his sleeves rolled up, carrying a pan of dirty dishwater. He stopped mid-motion, about to empty the pan, when he spotted Weedon Scott petting White Fang.

At the moment his voice shattered the quiet, White Fang sprang backward, growling fiercely at him.

Matt looked at his boss with hurt disapproval.

"If you don't mind me expressing my feelings, Mr. Scott, I'll freely say you're seventeen kinds of a damn fool and all of them different, and then some."

Weedon Scott smiled with a knowing look, stood up, and

walked over to White Fang. He spoke to him in gentle, calming tones, though only briefly, then carefully extended his hand, placed it on White Fang's head, and continued the petting that had been interrupted. White Fang tolerated it, keeping his gaze fixed warily, not on the man who was stroking him, but on the man who remained standing in the doorway.

"You might be the best mining expert around, sure enough," the dog-sled driver said with authority, "but you missed the opportunity of a lifetime when you were a boy and didn't run away to join a circus."

White Fang growled when he heard his voice, but this time he didn't jump away from the hand that was gently stroking his head and the back of his neck with long, calming movements.

This marked the start of White Fang's transformation—the conclusion of his former existence and the end of hatred's dominance. A new and mysteriously better life was beginning to emerge. Weedon Scott needed considerable thought and unlimited patience to make this happen. For White Fang, nothing short of a complete transformation was necessary. He needed to disregard the impulses and signals of instinct and logic, resist experience, and contradict life as he knew it.

Life as he had experienced it not only had no room for much of what he was now doing, but all the forces had worked against those he was now giving himself over to. In essence, when everything was taken into account, he needed to achieve a complete reorientation far more extensive than the one he had accomplished when he voluntarily came in from the wilderness and accepted Grey Beaver as his master. At that time he was just a young puppy, soft from creation, without shape, ready for the hand of circumstances to begin shaping him. But now things were different. The hand of circumstances had done its job all too thoroughly. Through it he had been molded and hardened into the Fighting Wolf, savage and merciless, incapable of love and impossible to love. To bring about this transformation was like a complete reversal of his very existence, and this at a time when the flexibility of youth was no longer available to him; when his inner fiber had become tough and gnarled; when the very fabric of his being had created an unbreakable texture, rough and inflexible; when the surface of his soul had turned to iron and all his instincts and principles had solidified into fixed patterns, wariness, hatred, and cravings.

Once more, in this fresh direction, it was the force of circumstances that pushed and guided him, softening what had grown rigid and reshaping it into a better form. Weedon Scott truly was this guiding force. He had reached the core of White Fang's character, and through kindness awakened abilities that had been dormant and nearly died out. One such ability was love. It replaced the simple liking that had been the strongest emotion he had ever felt in his relationships with humans.

But this love didn't develop overnight. It started as simple liking and gradually grew from there. White Fang chose not to run away, even though he was free to roam, because he genuinely liked this new master. This life was definitely an improvement over his existence in Beauty Smith's cage, and he needed to have some kind of master. Being ruled by humans was part of his essential nature. The mark of his dependence on people had been permanently etched into him on that early day when he turned away from the wilderness and crawled to Grey Beaver's feet to accept the beating he knew was coming. This mark had been pressed into him once more, this time permanently, when he returned from the wild a second time, after the long period of starvation had ended and fish were plentiful again in Grey Beaver's village.

And so, because he needed a god and because he preferred Weedon Scott to Beauty Smith, White Fang stayed. To show his loyalty, he took on the responsibility of protecting his master's property. He patrolled around the cabin while the sled dogs slept, and the first person who visited the cabin at night had to fight him off with a club until Weedon Scott came to help. But White Fang quickly learned to tell the difference between thieves and honest people, to judge the real meaning of how someone walked and carried themselves. The person who traveled with loud steps, walking straight to the cabin door, he left alone—though he watched him carefully until the door opened and he got approval from his master. But the person who moved quietly, taking roundabout paths, looking around cautiously, trying to stay hidden—that was the person who received no benefit of the doubt from White Fang, and who left suddenly, quickly, and without any dignity.

Weedon Scott had given himself the mission of saving White Fang—or more accurately, of saving humanity from the harm it had inflicted upon White Fang. This was a question of principle and moral duty. He believed that the damage done to White Fang was a debt owed by mankind and that it had to be repaid. Therefore, he made special efforts to be particularly gentle with the Fighting Wolf. Every day he made sure to stroke and comfort White Fang, and to spend considerable time doing so.

Initially wary and aggressive, White Fang came to enjoy this gentle touch. However, there was one behavior he could never abandon—his growling. He would growl continuously, from the moment the petting started until it finished. Yet this growl carried a different quality than before. A stranger wouldn't detect this subtle change, and to an outsider, White Fang's growling appeared as a display of primitive wildness that was both unnerving and terrifying. White Fang's throat had grown rough and coarse from years of producing fierce sounds, dating back to his first small snarl of rage as a cub in his den, and he couldn't soften those throat sounds now to convey the tenderness he actually felt. Even so, Weedon Scott possessed the sensitivity and understanding to perceive the new quality nearly lost within the ferocity—a quality that was the slightest suggestion of a contented murmur that only he could detect.

As time passed, his growing fondness quickly deepened into love. White Fang started to become conscious of this change, though he didn't understand what love actually was. He experienced it as an emptiness inside himself—a desperate, painful longing that demanded to be satisfied. It caused him suffering and restlessness, and he found relief only when his new master was near. During those moments, love brought him happiness, a fierce and exhilarating contentment. However, when separated from his master, the pain and anxiety returned; the emptiness within him expanded and overwhelmed him with its hollowness, while the craving ate away at him relentlessly.

White Fang was discovering who he truly was. Despite his mature age and the harsh, unyielding circumstances that had shaped him, his inner nature was expanding. Strange feelings and unfamiliar impulses were growing within him. His old way of behaving was transforming. In the past, he had sought comfort and relief from pain, avoided discomfort and suffering, and had acted accordingly. But now things were different. Because of this new emotion inside him, he often chose discomfort and pain for the sake of his master. So, in the early morning, instead of wandering and hunting for food, or resting in a protected spot, he would wait for hours on the cold cabin steps just to catch a glimpse of his master's face. At night, when his master came home, White Fang would leave the warm sleeping spot he had dug in the snow to receive the friendly snap of fingers and a word of welcome. Food, even food itself, he would give up to be with his master, to receive affection from him or to go with him down into the town.

Like had been replaced by love. And love was the plummet that dropped down into the depths of him where like had never reached. And in response from his depths had come this new thing—love. What was given to him, he gave back in return. This was truly a god, a god of love, a warm and glowing god, in whose light White Fang's nature blossomed as a flower blooms under the sun.

But White Fang wasn't one to show his feelings openly. He was too old, too set in his ways, to become skilled at expressing himself differently. He was too self-controlled, too deeply rooted in his own solitude. For too long he had practiced being reserved, distant, and sullen. He had never barked in his entire life, and he couldn't learn now to bark a greeting when his master came near. He never got in the way, never acted excessive or silly when showing his affection. He never rushed forward to meet his master. He would wait from a distance; but he always waited, was always present. His love had the quality of reverence, silent, wordless, a quiet devotion. Only through the constant gaze of his eyes did he show his love, and through the continuous tracking with his eyes of his master's every move. Sometimes, too, when his master looked at him and spoke to him, he revealed an uncomfortable self-awareness, brought on by his love's struggle to show itself and his physical inability to express it.

He learned to adapt himself in numerous ways to his new way of living. It became clear to him that he had to leave his master's dogs alone. However, his commanding nature made itself known, and he first had to beat them into recognizing his dominance and authority. Once this was achieved, he experienced little difficulty with them. They moved out of his way when he arrived and departed or moved among them, and when he imposed his will they followed his orders.

In the same way, he learned to accept Matt—as something that belonged to his master. His master seldom gave him food. Matt handled that responsibility, it was his job; yet White Fang understood that it was his master's food he consumed and that it was his master who fed him through Matt. Matt was the one who attempted to put him in the harness and make him pull the sled alongside the other dogs. But Matt was unsuccessful. It wasn't until Weedon Scott placed the harness on White Fang and trained him that he grasped what was expected. He interpreted it as his master's desire that Matt should control him and put him to work just as he controlled and worked his master's other dogs.

The Mackenzie toboggans were different from the Klondike sleds, which had runners underneath them. The way of controlling the dogs was also different. The team didn't work in a fan formation. Instead, the dogs worked in a single line, one after another, pulling on double traces. And here in the Klondike, the leader truly was the leader. The smartest and strongest dog became the leader, and the rest of the team both obeyed and feared him. It was bound to happen that White Fang would quickly claim this position. He couldn't settle for anything less, as Matt discovered after dealing with much hassle and difficulty. White Fang chose this role for himself, and Matt supported his decision with colorful language after they had tested it out. However, even though he worked pulling the sled during the day, White Fang didn't give up protecting his master's belongings at night. This meant he was working around the clock, always alert and loyal, making him the most precious of all the dogs.

"Speaking freely about what's on my mind," Matt said one day, "I have to say that you were really smart when you paid what you did for that dog. You completely outsmarted Beauty Smith on top of punching him in the face."

A fresh wave of anger flashed in Weedon Scott's grey eyes, and he muttered fiercely, "The beast!"

In the late spring, a great trouble came to White Fang. Without warning, the love-master disappeared. There had been warning, but White Fang was inexperienced in such things and did not understand the packing of a suitcase. He remembered afterwards that this packing had preceded the master's disappearance; but at the time he suspected nothing. That night he waited for the master to return. At midnight the cold wind that blew drove him to shelter at the back of the cabin. There he dozed, only half asleep, his ears alert for the first sound of the familiar footstep. But, at two in the morning, his anxiety drove him out to the cold front porch, where he crouched, and waited.

But no master came. When morning arrived, the door opened and Matt stepped outside. White Fang looked at him with longing eyes. There was no shared language through which he could discover what he desperately needed to know. Days passed one after another, but still the master never appeared. White Fang, who had never experienced illness in his entire life, fell sick. He grew extremely ill, so severely that Matt was eventually forced to carry him inside the cabin. Additionally, when writing to his employer, Matt added a postscript about White Fang.

Weedon Scott, reading the letter down in Circle City, came across the following:

"That damn wolf won't work. Won't eat. Doesn't have any spirit left. All the dogs are picking on him. He wants to know what happened to you, and I don't know how to tell him. Maybe he's going to die."

Matt's words proved accurate. White Fang had stopped eating, become dejected, and let every dog in the team beat him up. Inside the cabin, he sprawled on the floor beside the stove, showing no interest in food, in Matt, or in living. Whether Matt spoke to him kindly or cursed at him made no difference; White Fang would only lift his lifeless eyes to look at the man briefly, then lower his head back to its usual spot resting on his front paws.

And then, one night, Matt was reading to himself, his lips moving as he mumbled the words, when a low whine from White Fang startled him. The dog had risen to his feet, ears pointed toward the door, listening with intense focus. A moment later, Matt heard a footstep. The door opened, and Weedon Scott walked in. The two men shook hands. Then Scott looked around the room.

"Where's the wolf?" he asked.

Then he found him, standing in the same spot where he had been lying down, close to the stove. He hadn't rushed forward like other dogs would have done. He stood there, watching and waiting.

"Holy smoke!" Matt exclaimed. "Look at him wag his tail!"

Weedon Scott walked halfway across the room toward him, calling his name at the same time. White Fang approached him, not with a huge leap, but still moving quickly. He snapped out of his self-awareness, but as he got closer, his eyes took on an unusual look. Something—an indescribable enormity of emotion—welled up in his eyes like light and radiated outward.

"He never looked at me like that the whole time you were gone!" Matt commented.

Weedon Scott didn't hear. He was crouched down on his heels, face to face with White Fang and stroking him—massaging the base of his ears, running long gentle strokes down his neck to his shoulders, lightly tapping his spine with his fingertips. And White Fang was growling in response, the melodic tone of his growl more distinct than ever.

But that wasn't everything. His overwhelming joy and the immense love within him, constantly rising and fighting to show itself, managed to discover a fresh way to express these feelings. He abruptly pushed his head forward and worked his way between his master's arm and torso. There, tucked away and concealed from sight except for his ears, no longer making growling sounds, he kept nuzzling and cuddling closer.

The two men looked at each other. Scott's eyes were shining.

"Wow!" said Matt in an awestruck voice.

A moment later, after he had pulled himself together, he said, "I always maintained that wolf was actually a dog. Just look at him!"

When the love-master came back, White Fang got better quickly. He stayed inside the cabin for two nights and one day.

Then he ventured outside. The sled dogs had forgotten how strong and skilled he was. They only remembered what had happened most recently, which was seeing him weak and sick. When they saw him coming out of the cabin, they attacked him.

"Talk about your brawls," Matt whispered with delight, standing in the doorway and watching.

"Give them hell, you wolf! Give them hell!—and then some!"

White Fang didn't need any encouragement. Having his beloved master back was more than enough. Life surged through him once more, magnificent and unstoppable. He fought purely from joy, discovering in the battle a way to express all the feelings inside him that he couldn't put into words. There could only be one outcome. The pack scattered in shameful defeat, and it wasn't until nightfall that the dogs came slinking back, one after another, showing through their meekness and submission that they acknowledged White Fang as their leader.

Having learned to snuggle, White Fang did it frequently. It was his ultimate gesture. He couldn't go any further than this. The one thing he had always been especially protective of was his head. He had never liked having it touched. It was his wild nature, the fear of being hurt and trapped, that had created those panicked urges to avoid contact. His instincts demanded that his head remain free. And now, with his beloved master, his snuggling was a conscious choice to put himself in a position of complete vulnerability. It was a display of total trust, of complete surrender, as if he were saying: "I place myself in your hands. Do with me whatever you wish."

One evening, shortly after they had returned, Scott and Matt were playing a game of cribbage before heading to bed. "Fifteen-two, fifteen-four and a pair makes six," Matt was counting as he moved his pegs, when suddenly there was shouting and the sound of growling outside. They glanced at each other as they began to get up from their seats.

"The wolf has killed someone," Matt said.

A wild scream of terror and agony urged them forward.

"Bring a light!" Scott shouted as he rushed outside.

Matt followed with the lamp, and in its glow they discovered a man lying on his back in the snow. His arms were crossed, one over the other, covering his face and throat. He was attempting to protect himself from White Fang's fangs. And protection was desperately needed. White Fang was furious, savagely attacking the most exposed area. From shoulder to wrist of the crossed arms, the coat sleeve, blue flannel shirt and undershirt were torn to shreds, while the arms themselves were horribly cut and bleeding profusely.

Both men witnessed everything in that first moment. In the next instant, Weedon Scott had grabbed White Fang by the throat and was pulling him away. White Fang fought and growled, but he didn't try to bite, and he quickly calmed down when his master spoke sharply to him.

Matt helped the man get back on his feet. As he stood up, he lowered his crossed arms, revealing the brutal face of Beauty Smith. The dog-musher immediately let go of him, reacting like someone who had just grabbed a burning coal. Beauty Smith squinted in the lamplight and looked around. When he spotted White Fang, terror flooded his face.

At that exact moment, Matt spotted two items lying in the snow. He brought the lamp closer to them, pointing them out with his toe for his boss to see—a steel dog chain and a heavy club.

Weedon Scott observed and gave a nod of understanding. No words were exchanged. The dog handler placed his hand on Beauty Smith's shoulder and turned him around to face the opposite direction. There was no need for any words to be said. Beauty Smith began to move.

In the meantime the love-master was gently stroking White Fang and speaking to him.

"Tried to steal you, eh? And you wouldn't have it! Well, well, he made a mistake, didn't he?"

"Must have thought he had hold of seventeen devils," the dog-musher chuckled.

White Fang remained agitated and bristling, continuing to growl as his fur gradually settled down, while a soft, distant rumbling sound grew stronger in his throat.

Part V

Chapter I: The Long Trail

Something was about to happen. White Fang could feel the approaching disaster before any clear signs appeared. In unclear ways, he sensed that change was coming. He didn't understand how or why, but he picked up on the approaching event from the gods themselves. In ways more subtle than they realized, they revealed their plans to the wolf-dog who lingered around the cabin steps, and who, despite never entering the cabin, understood what was happening in their minds.

"Listen to that, will you!" the dog-musher shouted during supper one evening.

Weedon Scott listened carefully. A soft, worried whine drifted through the door, resembling muffled sobbing that had just become loud enough to hear. This was followed by a long, deliberate sniff as White Fang confirmed to himself that his master remained inside and hadn't mysteriously disappeared on one of his solitary departures.

"I really think that wolf has figured you out," the dog-musher said.

Weedon Scott glanced over at his companion with eyes that seemed to beg for understanding, even though his spoken words suggested otherwise.

"What the hell am I supposed to do with a wolf in California?" he demanded.

"That's exactly what I'm saying," Matt replied. "What on earth can you do with a wolf in California?"

But this didn't satisfy Weedon Scott. The other man appeared to be evaluating him in a detached, noncommittal manner.

"White men's dogs wouldn't stand a chance against him," Scott continued. "He would kill them immediately upon seeing them. If he didn't ruin me financially with lawsuits for damages, the authorities would confiscate him from me and put him to death by electrocution."

"He's an outright killer, I'm certain of it," the dog-musher remarked.

Weedon Scott eyed him with suspicion.

"It would never work," he said with certainty.

"That would never work!" Matt agreed. "You'd have to hire someone specifically just to take care of them."

The other person's suspicion was put to rest. He nodded with a cheerful expression. In the quiet that came after, they could hear the soft, half-crying whimper at the door, followed by a long, searching sniff.

"There's no denying he thinks a hell of a lot of you," Matt said.

"The other man stared at him with sudden anger. "Damn it all! I know my own mind and what's best for me!"

"I agree with you, but..."

"Only what?" Scott snapped.

"Only . . . " the dog-musher started quietly, then reconsidered and revealed his own growing irritation. "Well, you don't need to get so incredibly worked up about it. Based on how you're acting, someone would think you couldn't make up your own mind."

Weedon Scott thought it over for a moment, then spoke more softly: "You're right, Matt. I don't know what I want, and that's the problem."

"Why, it would be completely ridiculous for me to bring that dog with me," he burst out after another moment of silence.

"I agree with you," Matt replied, and once again his employer wasn't entirely satisfied with his response.

"But how in the world he knows you're going is what puzzles me," the dog-musher continued innocently.

"I don't understand it, Matt," Scott replied, shaking his head sadly.

Then came the day when White Fang saw the dreaded suitcase on the floor through the open cabin door, and his beloved master packing belongings into it. There was also constant movement back and forth, and the once peaceful atmosphere of the cabin was disturbed by strange upheaval and restlessness. This was unmistakable proof. White Fang had already sensed it through smell. Now he understood it logically. His god was getting ready for another departure. And since he hadn't been taken along before, he could now expect to be left behind again.

That night he raised his long, mournful howl. Just as he had howled in his younger days when he ran back from the wilderness to the village only to discover it had disappeared, with nothing but a pile of debris marking where Grey Beaver's tepee once stood, he now lifted his snout toward the cold stars and shared his sorrow with them.

Inside the cabin, the two men had just gone to bed.

"He's stopped eating again," Matt said from his bunk.

There was a grunt from Weedon Scott's bunk, and a rustling of blankets.

"Based on how upset he got the last time you left, I wouldn't be surprised if he died this time."

The blankets in the other bunk moved restlessly.

"Oh, shut up!" Scott shouted into the darkness. "You complain more than anyone I know."

"I agree with you," the dog-musher replied, and Weedon Scott wasn't entirely certain whether the other man had chuckled or not.

The following day, White Fang's worry and unease became even more intense. He followed closely behind his master whenever he stepped outside the cabin, and lingered anxiously on the front porch when his master stayed indoors. Through the open doorway, he could see pieces of luggage scattered across the floor. The suitcase had been accompanied by two large canvas bags and a wooden crate. Matt was busy wrapping the master's blankets and fur coat inside a small waterproof covering. White Fang whimpered softly as he observed this activity.

Later, two Indians showed up. White Fang observed them carefully as they picked up the luggage and followed Matt down the hill, who was carrying the bedding and the suitcase. However, White Fang didn't go with them. His master remained inside the cabin. After some time had passed, Matt came back. The master appeared at the door and called for White Fang to come inside.

"You poor thing," he said softly, stroking White Fang's ears and patting his back. "I'm heading down the long trail, old friend, where you can't come with me. Now give me a growl—one last, good farewell growl."

But White Fang wouldn't growl. Instead, after giving a longing, questioning look, he nestled close, burying his head out of sight between his master's arm and body.

"There she blows!" Matt shouted. From the Yukon came the rough, thundering sound of a river steamboat. "You need to wrap this up quickly. Make sure you lock the front door. I'll head out through the back. Hurry up!"

The two doors slammed shut at exactly the same time, and Weedon Scott stood waiting for Matt to walk around to the front. From behind the door came a soft whining and sobbing sound. This was followed by long, deep sniffs.

"You need to take good care of him, Matt," Scott said as they began walking down the hill. "Write to me and let me know how he's doing."

"Sure," the dog-musher replied. "But listen to that, will you!"

Both men came to a halt. White Fang was howling the way dogs howl when their masters are dead. He was expressing complete despair, his cry erupting upward in powerful, heartbreaking surges, fading into trembling anguish, then erupting upward once more with wave after wave of sorrow.

The Aurora was the first steamboat of the year heading to the Outside, and her decks were packed with successful adventurers and defeated gold seekers, all just as desperate to reach the Outside as they had originally been to get to the Inside. Near the gangplank, Scott was shaking hands with Matt, who was getting ready to go ashore. But Matt's hand went slack in the other's grip as his eyes darted past and stayed focused on something behind him. Scott turned to look. Sitting on the deck several feet away and watching longingly was White Fang.

The sled dog driver cursed quietly, his voice filled with amazement. Scott could only stare in astonishment.

"Did you lock the front door?" Matt asked urgently. The other person nodded and replied, "What about the back door?"

"You can bet I did," came the passionate response.

White Fang pressed his ears flat against his head in a submissive gesture, but he stayed right where he was, making no move to come closer.

"I'll have to take him ashore with me."

Matt took a few steps toward White Fang, but White Fang moved away from him. The dog-musher lunged forward quickly, and White Fang darted between the legs of several men standing nearby. Crouching low, spinning around, and changing direction suddenly, he moved across the deck, avoiding Matt's attempts to catch him.

But when the love-master spoke, White Fang came to him with immediate obedience.

"Won't come to the hand that's been feeding him all these months," the dog handler muttered with resentment. "And you—you've never fed him after those first few days when you were getting to know each other. I'll be damned if I can figure out how he's decided that you're the one in charge."

Scott, who had been petting White Fang, suddenly leaned in closer and pointed out freshly made cuts on his muzzle, and a gash between his eyes.

Matt leaned down and ran his hand along White Fang's stomach.

"We completely forgot about the window. He's all cut and gouged underneath. Must have butted clean through it, by gosh!"

But Weedon Scott wasn't paying attention. His mind was racing with thoughts. The Aurora's whistle blew one last warning that it was about to leave. Men were hurrying down the gangplank to get back on shore. Matt untied the bandana from around his neck and began putting it around White Fang's. Scott grabbed the dog-musher's hand.

"Goodbye, Matt, old friend. About the wolf—you don't need to write. You see, I've . . . !"

"What!" the dog-musher burst out. "You can't be serious . . .?"

"That's exactly what I mean. Here's your bandana. I'll write to you about him."

Matt stopped halfway down the gangplank.

"He'll never survive the climate!" he yelled back. "Not unless you shear him during warm weather!"

The gangplank was pulled in, and the Aurora moved away from the shore. Weedon Scott waved one final goodbye. Then he turned and leaned down toward White Fang, who was standing beside him.

"Now growl, damn you, growl," he said, as he gently patted the dog's responsive head and rubbed its ears that flattened under his touch.

Chapter II: The Southland

White Fang stepped off the steamship in San Francisco. He was overwhelmed. Deep within him, beneath any logical thought or conscious awareness, he had connected power with divinity. And never had the white men appeared to be such incredible gods as they did now, when he walked on the slippery pavement of San Francisco. The log cabins he had known were now replaced by soaring buildings. The streets were filled with dangers—wagons, carts, automobiles; massive, powerful horses pulling enormous trucks; and enormous cable and electric cars honking and clanging through the chaos, shrieking their relentless threat in the same way as the lynxes he had known in the northern wilderness.

All of this displayed raw power. Throughout everything, behind everything, stood humanity, ruling and controlling, expressing itself as it always had through dominance over the physical world. It was massive, overwhelming. White Fang felt awestruck. Fear gripped him. Just as during his puppyhood he had been forced to recognize his insignificance and weakness the day he first emerged from the wilderness into Grey Beaver's village, so now, despite his full-grown size and confident strength, he was made to feel tiny and helpless. And there were countless gods! The swarms of them made his head spin. The roar of the streets pounded his ears. He felt confused by the enormous and never-ending rush and motion of everything around him. More than ever before, he sensed his reliance on his love-master, staying close behind him no matter what occurred, never letting him out of his sight.

But White Fang would only catch a nightmarish glimpse of the city—an experience like a terrible dream, surreal and frightening, that would haunt his sleep for a long time afterward. His master placed him in a baggage car, chaining him to a corner surrounded by stacked trunks and suitcases. In this space, a short and muscular god ruled with tremendous noise, throwing trunks and boxes around, hauling them through the door and hurling them onto piles, or flinging them out the door with loud crashes and bangs to other gods waiting below.

In this chaotic mess of luggage, White Fang found himself abandoned by his master. Or at least White Fang believed he had been abandoned, until he caught the scent of his master's canvas travel bags nearby, and then positioned himself to stand guard over them.

"'About time you showed up," grumbled the freight car attendant an hour later when Weedon Scott appeared at the door. "That dog of yours won't let me touch any of your belongings."

White Fang stepped out of the car. He was amazed. The terrifying city had vanished. To him, the car had been nothing more than a room inside a house, and when he had gotten into it, the city had surrounded him completely. During that time, the city had disappeared. Its thunderous noise no longer pounded in his ears. Spread out before him was pleasant countryside, bathed in sunlight and peaceful in its calm. However, he had little opportunity to wonder at this change. He accepted it just as he accepted all the mysterious actions and displays of the gods. This was simply their way.

There was a carriage waiting. A man and a woman walked up to the master. The woman reached out her arms and grabbed the master around the neck—an aggressive move! In the next instant, Weedon Scott had broken free from her embrace and rushed to White Fang, who had transformed into a growling, furious beast.

"It's all right, mother," Scott said as he held White Fang firmly and calmed him down. "He thought you were going to hurt me, and he wouldn't allow it. It's all right. It's all right. He'll learn soon enough."

"And in the meantime I may be allowed to love my son when his dog isn't around," she laughed, though she was pale and weak from the shock.

She looked at White Fang, who growled and raised his fur while staring with hostile intent.

"He'll have to learn, and he will, without delay," Scott said.

He spoke gently to White Fang until the dog had calmed down, then his voice grew firm.

"Get down, sir! Get down!"

White Fang had learned this lesson from his master, and he followed the command, even though he settled down with obvious reluctance and resentment.

"Now, mother."

Scott opened his arms to her, but kept his eyes on White Fang.

"Get down!" he warned. "Get down!"

White Fang bristled quietly, crouching halfway as he stood up, then settled back down and watched the threatening action happen again. However, nothing bad came from it, or from the hug that the unfamiliar man-god gave afterward. The suitcases were then loaded into the carriage, the strange gods and his beloved master climbed in, and White Fang followed along, sometimes running alertly behind, sometimes bristling as he approached the galloping horses to warn them that he was watching to make sure no harm came to the god they were pulling so quickly across the ground.

After fifteen minutes, the carriage turned through a stone gateway and continued between two rows of arched, intertwining walnut trees. Expansive lawns stretched out on both sides, their wide expanse interrupted occasionally by massive, thick-branched oak trees. In the nearby distance, sun-bleached hay fields displayed shades of tan and gold, contrasting sharply with the fresh green of the well-maintained grass, while the golden-brown hills and highland meadows lay beyond. From the top of the lawn, positioned on the first gentle rise above the valley floor, the house gazed down with its deep porch and numerous windows.

Little opportunity was given to White Fang to observe all of this. The carriage had barely entered the grounds when a sheep-dog confronted him—bright-eyed, sharp-muzzled, righteously indignant and furious. The dog positioned itself between White Fang and his master, blocking his path. White Fang gave no warning snarl, but his fur bristled as he launched into his silent and lethal charge. This attack was never finished. He stopped with clumsy suddenness, his stiff front legs bracing against his forward momentum, nearly dropping onto his hindquarters in his desperation to avoid contact with the dog he had been about to strike. The sheep-dog was female, and the natural law of his species created an insurmountable barrier between them. For him to attack her would demand nothing short of betraying his deepest instincts.

But the sheep-dog was different. Since she was female, she didn't have that same instinct. However, as a sheep-dog, her natural fear of the wilderness, particularly of wolves, was exceptionally sharp. To her, White Fang represented a wolf—the ancient enemy that had hunted her ancestors' flocks since the earliest days when sheep were first gathered and protected by her distant forebears. Therefore, when he stopped his charge toward her and steadied himself to prevent collision, she leaped at him. He growled instinctively as her teeth sank into his shoulder, but he made no attempt to harm her beyond that reaction. He retreated awkwardly, his legs stiff with embarrassment, and attempted to move around her. He weaved back and forth, circling and turning, but it was useless. She consistently positioned herself between him and wherever he was trying to go.

"Here, Collie!" called the strange man in the carriage.

Weedon Scott laughed.

"Don't worry about it, father. It's good training for him. White Fang will need to learn many things, and it's better that he starts now. He'll adapt just fine."

The carriage continued moving forward, and Collie still stood in White Fang's path. He attempted to get past her by abandoning the driveway and running in a circle across the grass, but she ran along the inner, tighter circle and was always positioned there, confronting him with her two rows of shining teeth. He circled back, crossing the driveway to the other side of the lawn, and once again she cut him off.

The carriage was taking the master away. White Fang caught brief glimpses of it vanishing among the trees. The situation was desperate. He attempted another circle. She followed, running quickly. And then, suddenly, he turned on her. It was his old fighting technique. Shoulder to shoulder, he hit her directly. Not only was she knocked down. She had been running so fast that she tumbled along, rolling on her back, then on her side, as she struggled to stop herself, scratching at the gravel with her feet and crying out sharply from her wounded pride and anger.

White Fang didn't hesitate. The path ahead was open, and that was exactly what he needed. She chased after him, her cries never stopping. Now it was a straight sprint, and when it came to true running, White Fang had lessons to teach her. She ran desperately, frantically, pushing herself to the limit, her every bound showing the tremendous effort she was putting forth: meanwhile White Fang glided effortlessly away from her in silence, moving like a phantom across the earth.

As he rounded the house toward the covered entrance, he came upon the carriage. It had come to a stop, and the master was getting out. At that moment, still running at full speed, White Fang suddenly became aware of an attack coming from his side. It was a deer-hound charging at him. White Fang tried to turn and face it. But he was moving too quickly, and the hound was too near. It slammed into his side; and because of his forward momentum and how unexpected the attack was, White Fang was thrown to the ground and tumbled completely over. He emerged from the confusion looking fierce and menacing, ears pressed flat against his head, lips curled back, nose wrinkled, his teeth snapping together as his fangs just barely missed the hound's vulnerable throat.

The master was running toward them, but he was too far away; it was Collie who saved the hound's life. Before White Fang could leap forward and deliver the killing blow, and just as he was about to spring, Collie arrived. She had been outmaneuvered and outrun, not to mention being rudely thrown into the gravel, and her arrival was like a tornado—filled with wounded pride, righteous anger, and instinctive hatred for this intruder from the wilderness. She hit White Fang from the side in the middle of his leap, and once again he was knocked down and sent tumbling.

The next moment the master arrived, and with one hand held White Fang, while the father called off the dogs.

"Well, this is quite a heated welcome for a poor solitary wolf from the Arctic," the master said, as White Fang settled down beneath his gentle touch. "In his entire life he's only been knocked down once before, and now he's been thrown to the ground twice in half a minute."

The carriage had departed, and other unfamiliar gods had emerged from the house. Several of these remained respectfully at a distance, but two of them, both women, committed the aggressive act of embracing the master around his neck. White Fang, nevertheless, was starting to accept this behavior. No damage appeared to result from it, and the sounds these gods produced were definitely not menacing. These gods also attempted to approach White Fang, but he drove them away with a growl, and the master similarly discouraged them with spoken words. During these moments White Fang pressed close against the master's legs and received comforting touches on his head.

The dog, following the command "Dick! Lie down, sir!" had climbed the steps and settled down on one side of the porch, continuing to growl while maintaining a hostile watch over the intruder. Collie had been taken under the care of one of the woman-gods, who wrapped her arms around the dog's neck and gently stroked and comforted her; however, Collie remained deeply confused and anxious, whimpering and unable to settle, disturbed by the tolerated presence of this wolf and certain that the gods were making an error.

All the gods climbed the steps to go into the house. White Fang stayed close behind his master's feet. Dick, standing on the porch, growled, and White Fang, positioned on the steps, raised his fur and growled in response.

"Take Collie inside and let the two of them settle this on their own," Scott's father suggested. "They'll be friends after that."

"Then White Fang, to show his friendship, will have to be chief mourner at the funeral," the master laughed.

The older Scott looked with disbelief, first at White Fang, then at Dick, and finally at his son.

"You mean . . .?"

Weedon nodded. "That's exactly what I mean. Dick would be dead within a minute—two minutes at most."

He turned to White Fang. "Come on, you wolf. It's you that'll have to come inside."

White Fang climbed the steps with stiff legs and crossed the porch, his tail standing straight up, keeping his eyes fixed on Dick to prevent any surprise attack from the side, while simultaneously preparing himself for whatever fierce unknown threat might leap out at him from inside the house. However, nothing frightening emerged, and once he made it indoors, he carefully explored the area, examining everything and finding no danger. He then settled down with a satisfied grunt at his master's feet, watching everything that happened around him, always ready to jump up and fight for his life against the terrors he believed must be hiding beneath the roof of this dwelling.

Chapter III: The God's Domain

White Fang was naturally adaptable, and his extensive travels had taught him the importance and necessity of adjusting to new situations. At Sierra Vista, the name of Judge Scott's estate, White Fang quickly started making himself comfortable. He experienced no more serious conflicts with the dogs. They understood the customs of the Southland gods better than he did, and in their view, he had proven himself worthy when he followed the gods into the house. Despite being a wolf, and though such a thing had never happened before, the gods had approved of his presence, and the dogs, being servants of the gods, had no choice but to accept this approval.

Dick was forced to go through some rigid formalities at the beginning, but afterward he peacefully accepted White Fang as a new resident of the property. If Dick had gotten his way, the two would have become close companions; however, White Fang had no interest in forming friendships. All he wanted from other dogs was to be left in peace. Throughout his entire life he had stayed distant from his own species, and he continued to want that separation. Dick's friendly advances annoyed him, so he growled at Dick to drive him away. In the north he had discovered the important rule that he must leave the master's dogs alone, and he hadn't forgotten that rule now. But he demanded his own solitude and isolation, and he so completely disregarded Dick that the friendly dog eventually gave up on him and barely paid him any more attention than he would the hitching post by the stable.

Collie felt differently. Although she accepted him because the gods demanded it, that didn't mean she had to leave him alone. Deep within her nature lay the memories of countless crimes he and his kind had committed against her ancestors. The destroyed sheep pens wouldn't be forgotten in a single day or even a generation. All of this drove her forward, pushing her toward revenge. She couldn't openly defy the gods who allowed his presence, but that didn't stop her from making his life miserable in small ways. An ancient feud existed between them, and she would make sure he never forgot it.

So Collie used her gender to her advantage, targeting White Fang and mistreating him. His natural instincts wouldn't allow him to attack her, while her relentless behavior made it impossible for him to simply ignore her presence. Whenever she charged at him, he would turn his fur-covered shoulder toward her sharp teeth and walk away with stiff legs and dignity. When she pushed him too far, he had no choice but to move in a circle, keeping his shoulder facing her direction while turning his head away, wearing a patient and weary expression on his face and in his eyes. Occasionally, though, a bite to his hindquarters would speed up his retreat and strip away any sense of dignity. Most of the time, however, he succeeded in maintaining a composure that bordered on ceremonial seriousness. He pretended she didn't exist whenever possible and made it his priority to stay out of her path. Whenever he spotted her approaching or heard her coming, he would stand up and walk away.

There was much for White Fang to learn about other aspects of life. Living in the Northland had been straightforward compared to the complex arrangements at Sierra Vista. Above all, he needed to understand his master's family. In some ways, he was ready for this challenge. Just as Mit-sah and Kloo-kooch had been part of Grey Beaver's household, sharing his meals, his warmth, and his sleeping place, now at Sierra Vista, everyone who lived in the house belonged to his beloved master.

But this situation was different, with many variations from what he had known before. Sierra Vista was a much larger and more complex place than Grey Beaver's tepee. There were numerous people he needed to understand. Judge Scott lived there, along with his wife. The master had two sisters named Beth and Mary. His wife Alice was part of the household, and then there were his young children, Weedon and Maud, who were four and six years old and still toddling around. Nobody could explain to him who all these people were, and he understood nothing about family connections and relationships, nor would he ever be able to grasp such concepts. However, he quickly figured out that all of these individuals belonged to his master in some way. Then, through careful watching whenever he had the chance, by studying their actions, their words, and even the subtle tones in their voices, he gradually learned how close each person was to the master and how much favor they held with him. Using this understanding as his guide, White Fang treated each person accordingly. Whatever the master valued, he valued as well; whatever was precious to the master was something White Fang would cherish and protect with great care.

This is how things went with the two children. Throughout his entire life, he had despised children. He detested and was afraid of their hands. The experiences he had endured regarding their domination and brutality during his time in the Indian villages had taught him harsh lessons. When Weedon and Maud first came near him, he growled as a warning and appeared threatening. A blow from his master and a stern command then forced him to allow their affection, though he continued to growl beneath their small hands, and his growling contained no gentle, soothing sound. Eventually, he noticed that the boy and girl held great importance in his master's regard. From that point on, no blow or harsh word was needed before they could stroke him.

White Fang was never overly affectionate in his displays of emotion. He submitted to his master's children with reluctant but genuine tolerance, putting up with their playful antics the way someone might endure a difficult medical procedure. When his patience reached its limit, he would rise and walk away from them with firm determination. However, as time passed, he actually began to enjoy the children's company. Even so, he remained reserved in his behavior. He wouldn't approach them on his own initiative. Instead of immediately leaving when he spotted them, though, he started waiting for them to come to him. Eventually, people began to notice that his eyes would brighten with pleasure when he saw them coming toward him, and that he would watch them leave with what seemed like wistful disappointment when they went off to find other entertainment.

All of this was a gradual process that required time to develop. After the children, Judge Scott held the next highest place in White Fang's affections. There were likely two reasons for this preference. First, Judge Scott was clearly someone the master valued greatly, and second, he wasn't overly expressive with his emotions. White Fang enjoyed lying at the judge's feet on the spacious porch while he read his newspaper, occasionally receiving a glance or a few words—simple gestures that showed he acknowledged White Fang's presence and recognized his existence. However, this only happened when the master wasn't present. Whenever the master appeared, everyone else simply disappeared from White Fang's awareness.

White Fang let every family member pet him and shower him with attention, but he never offered them what he gave to his master. Their gentle touches couldn't bring forth the loving rumble from his throat, and no matter how hard they tried, they could never convince him to curl up close against them. This display of complete letting go and submission, of total trust, he saved only for his master. In truth, he never saw the family members as anything more than belongings of the love-master.

White Fang had also learned early on to distinguish between the family members and the household servants. The servants were frightened of him, while he simply chose not to attack them.

This was because he viewed them as belonging to the master, just like other possessions. Between White Fang and the servants, there existed only neutrality and nothing more. They prepared meals for the master, cleaned the dishes, and performed other duties just as Matt had done back in the Klondike. They were, essentially, part of the household's equipment.

Outside the household, White Fang had even more to discover and understand. His master's territory was vast and complicated, but it still had clear boundaries and limits. The land ended at the county road. Beyond that lay the shared territory of all gods—the roads and streets. Then, behind other fences, were the specific territories belonging to other gods. Countless rules controlled all these areas and dictated behavior; however, he couldn't understand the language of the gods, and there was no way for him to learn except through direct experience. He followed his instinctive urges until they conflicted with some rule. After this happened several times, he understood the rule and from then on followed it.

The most powerful part of his education came from the master's gentle slap and the disapproval in the master's voice. White Fang loved his master so deeply that even a light tap from him caused more pain than any harsh beating he had received from Grey Beaver or Beauty Smith. Those men had only damaged his body; underneath the physical wounds, his spirit had remained fierce and unbroken. However, when the master struck him, the blow was always too gentle to cause physical harm. Still, it cut much deeper. It showed that the master was disappointed in him, and White Fang's spirit crumbled under that knowledge.

In reality, physical punishment was seldom used. The master's voice alone was enough. Through it, White Fang understood whether his behavior was right or wrong. He used it to guide his conduct and modify his actions. It served as his compass, helping him navigate and understand the customs of this new land and way of life.

In the Northland, the dog was the only animal that had been tamed by humans. Every other creature roamed free in the wilderness, and unless they were too dangerous to handle, any dog could rightfully hunt them for food. Throughout his entire life, White Fang had searched among living creatures to find his meals. It never occurred to him that things worked differently in the Southland. However, he would discover this truth soon after arriving in Santa Clara Valley. While wandering casually around the corner of the house early one morning, he stumbled upon a chicken that had broken free from its coop. White Fang's instinctive reaction was to devour it. With just a few quick leaps, a snap of his jaws, and one terrified cry from the bird, he had caught the wandering chicken. The bird was raised on the farm and was plump and succulent; White Fang licked his lips and concluded that this type of meal was excellent.

Later that day, he came across another loose chicken near the stables. One of the stable workers rushed to help. He didn't know what breed White Fang was, so he grabbed a light buggy whip as his weapon. When the whip first struck, White Fang turned away from the chicken and focused on the man. A club might have stopped White Fang, but a whip wouldn't. Without making a sound or showing any sign of pain, he took a second lash as he charged forward, and when he lunged for the man's throat, the groom shouted, "My God!" and stumbled backward. He let go of the whip and threw his arms up to protect his throat. As a result, his forearm was torn open down to the bone.

The man was terrified. What truly unsettled the groom wasn't so much White Fang's viciousness as it was his complete silence. Still shielding his throat and face with his torn and bloodied arm, he attempted to back away toward the barn. Things would have ended badly for him if Collie hadn't arrived at that moment. Just as she had rescued Dick's life before, she now came to the groom's rescue. She charged at White Fang with wild fury. Her instincts had been correct. She had understood the situation better than the foolish humans. All her doubts and concerns were now proven right. Here was the old predator returning to his former ways once again.

The groom ran away to the stables, and White Fang retreated from Collie's fierce teeth, or turned his shoulder toward them and moved in circles. However, Collie didn't stop after a reasonable period of punishment, as she usually did. Instead, she became increasingly excited and furious with each passing moment, until finally, White Fang abandoned all dignity and openly ran away from her across the fields.

"He'll learn to stop bothering the chickens," the master said. "But I can't teach him that lesson until I catch him doing it."

Two nights later, the deed took place, but on a much larger scale than the master had expected. White Fang had carefully studied the chicken coops and observed how the chickens behaved. During the night, after the birds had settled in to sleep, he climbed up a stack of freshly delivered lumber. From that position, he reached the roof of a chicken coop, crossed over the peak, and dropped down to the ground inside the enclosure. Moments later, he was inside the building, and the killing began.

In the morning, when the master stepped onto the porch, fifty white Leghorn hens, arranged in a line by the stable hand, met his gaze. He whistled quietly to himself, first in shock, and then finally in amazement. White Fang also caught his attention, but the dog showed no trace of shame or guilt. He held himself proudly, as if he had accomplished something worthy of praise and honor. There was no awareness of wrongdoing about him. The master's mouth grew tight as he confronted the unpleasant duty ahead. Then he spoke sternly to the oblivious offender, and his voice carried nothing but divine fury. He also pressed White Fang's nose down against the dead hens, while giving him a thorough beating at the same time.

White Fang never attacked a chicken coop again. It was forbidden, and he had understood this rule. Then his master brought him into the chicken yards. When White Fang saw the living prey fluttering around him and right beneath his nose, his natural instinct was to pounce on it. He followed this instinct, but his master's voice stopped him. They stayed in the yards for thirty minutes. Again and again the urge overwhelmed White Fang, and each time he gave in to it, his master's voice held him back. This is how he learned the rule, and before he left the chickens' territory, he had learned to pay no attention to them at all.

"You can never cure a chicken-killer." Judge Scott shook his head sadly at the lunch table when his son told him about the lesson he had taught White Fang. "Once they develop the habit and get a taste for blood..." He shook his head sadly once more.

"But Weedon Scott didn't agree with his father. "I'll tell you what I'll do," he said with determination. "I'll lock White Fang in with the chickens for the entire afternoon."

"But think of the chickens," objected the judge.

"And furthermore," the son continued, "for every chicken he kills, I'll pay you one gold dollar."

"But you should punish father, too," Beth interrupted.

Her sister backed her up, and a wave of agreement swept around the table. Judge Scott nodded in approval.

"All right." Weedon Scott thought for a moment. "And if, by the end of the afternoon White Fang hasn't hurt a single chicken, for every ten minutes he's been in the yard, you'll need to tell him, seriously and carefully, just as if you were sitting as a judge and making an official ruling, 'White Fang, you are smarter than I thought.'"

From hidden spots around the property, the family observed what was happening. However, the whole thing turned out to be a complete disappointment. Trapped in the yard and then abandoned by his owner, White Fang simply lay down and fell asleep. At one point he stood up and walked over to the water trough to get a drink. He paid no attention whatsoever to the chickens. As far as he was concerned, they simply weren't there. At four o'clock he made a running leap, reached the top of the chicken coop and jumped down to the ground on the other side, from where he walked calmly back to the house. He had understood the rule. And there on the porch, in front of the thrilled family, Judge Scott stood face to face with White Fang and said slowly and seriously, sixteen times, "White Fang, you are smarter than I thought."

The sheer number of rules confused White Fang and frequently got him into trouble. He needed to understand that he couldn't touch the chickens that other gods owned. There were also cats, rabbits, and turkeys—he had to leave all of them alone. Actually, when he had only partially grasped these rules, he got the impression that he should avoid all living creatures. Out in the back pasture, a quail could take flight right in front of his face without being harmed. Though every muscle was taut and he trembled with anticipation and longing, he controlled his natural impulses and remained motionless. He was following the commands of the gods.

And then, one day, while out in the back pasture again, he watched Dick chase after a jackrabbit. The master stood there observing and chose not to step in. In fact, he urged White Fang to participate in the pursuit. Through this experience, he discovered that jackrabbits weren't off-limits. Eventually, he figured out the complete rule. He must not show hostility toward any domestic animals. If friendship wasn't possible, then at least he had to remain neutral. However, the other creatures—the squirrels, quail, and cottontails—were wild animals that had never submitted to human authority. Any dog could rightfully hunt them. Only the domesticated animals received protection from the gods, and deadly conflict among the tame was forbidden. The gods controlled life and death for their subjects, and they guarded this power jealously.

Life in the Santa Clara Valley was complicated after the simple ways of the Northland. The most important thing these complex civilized ways required was control and restraint—a balance of self that was as delicate as floating spider silk and yet as unbending as steel. Life showed a thousand different faces, and White Fang discovered he had to face them all—like when he traveled to town, into San Jose, running behind the carriage or wandering the streets when the carriage came to a stop. Life streamed past him, deep and broad and diverse, constantly pressing against his senses, requiring immediate and constant adjustments and responses from him, and forcing him, almost always, to hold back his natural instincts.

There were butcher shops with meat hanging within easy reach. He wasn't allowed to touch this meat. There were cats at the houses his master visited that he had to leave alone. And there were dogs everywhere that growled at him, but he couldn't fight back. Then, on the busy sidewalks, there were countless people who noticed him. They would stop and stare at him, point him out to each other, look him over, talk about him, and worst of all, pet him. He had to put up with all these risky encounters with so many unfamiliar hands. But he managed to endure it all. What's more, he stopped being clumsy and self-aware. He began to accept the attention from all these strange gods in a dignified way. He graciously allowed their attempts at friendliness. At the same time, there was something about him that kept people from getting too familiar. They would pat him on the head and move on, satisfied and proud of their own boldness.

However, life wasn't entirely simple for White Fang. While running behind the carriage on the outskirts of San Jose, he came across some small boys who regularly threw stones at him. Still, he understood that he wasn't allowed to chase after them and bring them down. In this situation, he was forced to go against his natural instinct for self-preservation, and go against it he did, because he was growing domesticated and preparing himself for civilization.

Nevertheless, White Fang wasn't completely happy with this situation. He didn't have any complex thoughts about what was right or wrong, or about fairness. However, there's a natural sense of what's fair that exists in all living things, and this instinct made him angry about the injustice of not being allowed to defend himself against those who threw stones at him. He had forgotten that in the agreement he had made with the gods, they had promised to take care of him and protect him. But one day his master jumped down from the carriage with a whip in his hand and gave the stone-throwers a beating. After that, they stopped throwing stones, and White Fang understood what had happened and felt satisfied.

White Fang had another similar experience. On his way to town, three dogs hung around the saloon at the crossroads and made it their habit to charge at him whenever he passed by. Since his master knew how deadly White Fang could be in a fight, he had constantly drilled into him the rule that he must never fight. Because White Fang had learned this lesson thoroughly, he found himself in a difficult position every time he walked past the crossroads saloon. After each initial attack, his growling would keep the three dogs at bay, but they would follow behind him, barking, quarreling, and taunting him. This situation continued for quite a while. The men at the saloon even encouraged the dogs to go after White Fang. One day they deliberately set the dogs on him. His master brought the carriage to a halt.

"Go to it," he said to White Fang.

But White Fang couldn't believe what he was seeing. He stared at the master, then shifted his gaze to the dogs. After that, he looked back at the master with eager, questioning eyes.

The master nodded his head. "Go to them, old fellow. Eat them up."

White Fang didn't hesitate any longer. He spun around and jumped silently into the midst of his enemies. All three dogs turned to face him. A fierce battle erupted with snarling and growling, snapping teeth, and a whirlwind of thrashing bodies. Dust from the road billowed up in a thick cloud, hiding the fight from view. After several minutes, two dogs lay struggling in the dirt while the third ran away as fast as it could. The fleeing dog jumped over a ditch, crashed through a wooden fence, and raced across an open field. White Fang gave chase, gliding over the ground with the smooth movement and speed of a wolf, quick and silent, and in the middle of the field he caught up to the dog and killed it.

With this triple killing, his main troubles with dogs came to an end. Word spread up and down the valley, and men made sure their dogs did not bother the Fighting Wolf.

Chapter IV: The Call of Kind

The months passed by one after another. Food was abundant and there was no labor required in the South, so White Fang lived well-fed, thriving, and content. He wasn't just physically located in the southern region, but he had also found himself in the springtime of his existence. The kindness shown by humans was like sunlight warming him, and he bloomed like a plant growing in rich, fertile earth.

And yet he stayed somehow different from other dogs. He understood the law even better than the dogs that had never known any other life, and he followed the law more carefully; but there was still something about him that hinted at hidden ferocity, as if the Wild still remained in him and the wolf within him was only sleeping.

He never formed friendships with other dogs. He had lived in isolation from his own species, and he would remain that way. During his early days as a puppy, suffering under the torment of Lip-lip and the pack of young dogs, and later during his fighting period with Beauty Smith, he had developed a deep-rooted hatred for other dogs. The normal path of his existence had been altered, and turning away from his own kind, he had attached himself to humans instead.

Besides, all Southland dogs viewed him with distrust. He triggered their instinctive fear of the wilderness, and they always welcomed him with snarls, growls, and hostile hatred. He, meanwhile, discovered that he didn't need to actually bite them. His bared fangs and curled lips worked consistently well, almost always succeeding in sending a charging, barking dog scrambling backward.

But there was one challenge in White Fang's life—Collie. She never left him alone for a single moment. She wasn't as willing to follow the rules as he was. She resisted all of the master's attempts to make her befriend White Fang. Her sharp and anxious snarl constantly filled his ears. She had never gotten over the incident when he killed the chickens, and she stubbornly maintained that his motives were evil. She assumed he was guilty before he even did anything wrong, and she acted toward him based on that assumption. She became a constant annoyance to him, like a police officer trailing him around the stable and the kennels, and if he so much as looked with curiosity at a pigeon or chicken, she would erupt into an angry outburst of rage and indignation. His preferred method of ignoring her was to lie down with his head resting on his front paws and pretend to be asleep. This always confused and quieted her.

With the exception of Collie, everything was going well for White Fang. He had learned self-control and composure, and he understood the rules. He developed steadiness, tranquility, and a philosophical acceptance of things. He no longer existed in a threatening environment. Danger, pain, and death weren't constantly lurking around him. Eventually, the unknown—as something terrifying and threatening that always seemed about to happen—disappeared. Life became gentle and comfortable. It moved along peacefully, with neither fear nor enemies waiting along the path.

He longed for the snow without realizing it. If he had actually thought about it, he would have considered it "an unusually long summer"; instead, he simply felt a vague, unconscious yearning for the snow. Similarly, particularly during the intense summer heat when the sun made him uncomfortable, he felt subtle desires for the northern regions. The only impact these feelings had on him, though, was to leave him feeling anxious and restless without understanding what was troubling him.

White Fang had never been one to show his feelings openly. Apart from cuddling close and adding a gentle rumbling sound to his affectionate growl, he possessed no other means of expressing his devotion. However, he was destined to find a third method. He had always been sensitive to the laughter of the gods. Their laughter had driven him to madness, filling him with wild fury. But he couldn't bring himself to feel anger toward his beloved master, and when this god chose to laugh at him in a kind, teasing manner, he found himself completely confused. He could sense the sharp pricks and stings of his old rage trying to surge within him, but it fought against his love. He couldn't feel angry; still, he needed to respond somehow. Initially, he maintained his dignity, which only made his master laugh even more. Then he attempted to become even more dignified, and his master's laughter grew louder than before. Eventually, his master's laughter completely dissolved his dignity. His jaws opened slightly, his lips curved upward a bit, and a puzzled look that contained more affection than amusement appeared in his eyes. He had discovered how to laugh.

In the same way, he learned to play roughly with the master, allowing himself to be knocked down and rolled around, becoming the target of countless playful tricks. In response, he would pretend to be angry, his fur standing on end as he growled fiercely and snapped his teeth together with what appeared to be murderous intent. However, he never lost control of himself. Those snaps always caught nothing but air. When these rough play sessions ended, after all the hitting and striking and snapping and snarling had reached a frenzied pace, they would suddenly stop and stand several feet away from each other, staring intensely. Then, just as abruptly, like sunshine breaking through storm clouds over the ocean, they would both start to laugh. This always ended with the master wrapping his arms around White Fang's neck and shoulders while White Fang made soft rumbling sounds and growled his song of affection.

But no one else ever played roughly with White Fang. He wouldn't allow it. He maintained his dignity, and when others tried to play with him, his threatening growl and raised fur were far from playful. Just because he permitted his master these freedoms didn't mean he should become an ordinary dog, showing affection to everyone, available to anyone for play and fun. He loved with complete devotion and refused to diminish himself or his love.

The master rode out on horseback frequently, and accompanying him became one of White Fang's primary responsibilities in life. In the Northland he had shown his loyalty by working hard in the harness; however, there were no sleds in the Southland, and dogs didn't carry loads on their backs there. Therefore, he demonstrated his loyalty in this new way by running alongside the master's horse. Even the longest day never exhausted White Fang. He possessed the wolf's natural stride— smooth, untiring, and effortless—and after covering fifty miles he would arrive energetically ahead of the horse.

It was during the horseback riding that White Fang developed another way of expressing himself—notable because he only did this twice in his entire life. The first instance happened when the master was attempting to train a high-spirited thoroughbred to open and close gates while keeping the rider mounted. Over and over again, he guided the horse toward the gate trying to get it to close, but each time the animal became scared and backed away, rearing and plunging. The horse grew increasingly nervous and agitated with every attempt. When it reared up on its hind legs, the master spurred it to bring its front legs back down to the ground, which only caused the horse to start kicking with its back legs. White Fang observed this scene with growing concern until he couldn't hold back any longer, at which point he leaped in front of the horse and barked fiercely in warning.

Though he frequently attempted to bark after that, and his master urged him on, he managed it only once, and even then his master wasn't there to witness it. A quick run across the field, a jackrabbit suddenly jumping up beneath the horse's hooves, a sharp swerve, a stumble, a crash to the ground, and a broken leg for his master—that's what caused it. White Fang lunged furiously at the throat of the horse that had caused the trouble, but his master's voice stopped him.

"Go home! Get yourself home!" the master ordered once he had determined the extent of his injury.

White Fang didn't want to leave him behind. The master considered writing a note, but when he searched through his pockets, he couldn't find a pencil or paper anywhere. Once more, he ordered White Fang to go home.

The dog looked at him longingly, pulled back, then came closer again and whimpered quietly. His owner spoke to him in a gentle but serious tone, and the dog perked up his ears, listening with intense concentration.

"That's fine, old friend, just head on home," the conversation went. "Go home and tell them what happened to me. Home with you, you wolf. Get going home!"

White Fang understood what "home" meant, and even though he couldn't grasp the rest of his master's words, he knew his master wanted him to go home. He turned around and reluctantly trotted away. Then he paused, uncertain, and glanced back over his shoulder.

"Go home!" came the sharp command, and this time he obeyed.

The family was sitting on the porch, enjoying the cool afternoon air, when White Fang showed up. He approached them, breathing heavily and covered in dust.

"Weedon's back," Weedon's mother announced.

The children greeted White Fang with joyful shouts and rushed toward him. He dodged them and moved along the porch, but they trapped him between a rocking chair and the railing. He snarled and attempted to force his way past them. Their mother watched nervously in their direction.

"I have to admit, he makes me anxious when he's around the children," she said. "I'm terrified that one day he'll suddenly turn on them without warning."

Snarling fiercely, White Fang leaped from the corner, knocking over both the boy and the girl. Their mother called them over to her side and consoled them, instructing them to leave White Fang alone.

"A wolf is a wolf!" Judge Scott remarked. "You can never trust one."

"But he's not completely ruthless," Beth interjected, defending her brother while he wasn't there to speak for himself.

"You only have Weedon's word on that," the judge replied. "He's just guessing that White Fang has some dog blood in him, but as he'll tell you himself, he doesn't really know anything about it. As for how he looks—"

He didn't complete what he was saying. White Fang stood in front of him, snarling aggressively.

"Go away! Lie down, sir!" Judge Scott commanded.

White Fang turned toward his beloved master's wife. She let out a terrified scream as he grabbed her dress with his teeth and pulled at it until the delicate material ripped apart. By now he had captured everyone's attention.

He had stopped growling and now stood upright, lifting his head to look directly into their faces. His throat moved in jerky, uncontrolled spasms, but no sound emerged, while his entire body struggled and writhed with the tremendous effort to express something that couldn't be put into words but desperately fought to be spoken.

"I hope he isn't losing his mind," said Weedon's mother. "I warned Weedon that I was concerned the hot climate wouldn't suit an Arctic animal."

"He's trying to speak, I think," Beth said.

At that moment, White Fang found his voice, erupting in a powerful burst of barking.

"Something has happened to Weedon," his wife said decisively.

They were all standing up now, and White Fang ran down the steps, glancing back for them to follow. For the second and final time in his life he had barked and made himself understood.

After this incident, he earned a special place in the hearts of everyone at Sierra Vista, and even the groom whose arm he had torn open acknowledged that he was an intelligent dog, despite being a wolf. Judge Scott maintained his original viewpoint and backed it up with measurements and detailed descriptions from encyclopedias and different natural history books, much to everyone's frustration.

The days passed one after another, pouring their endless sunshine across the Santa Clara Valley. But as the days grew shorter and White Fang's second winter in the Southland approached, he made an unusual discovery. Collie's teeth were no longer sharp. Her nips had become playful, with a gentleness that kept them from actually hurting him. He forgot that she had once made his life miserable, and when she played around him, he responded seriously, trying to be playful but only managing to look foolish.

One day she led him on a long chase through the back pasture into the woods. It was the afternoon when the master was supposed to go riding, and White Fang knew it. The horse stood saddled and ready at the door. White Fang hesitated. But there was something in him deeper than all the rules he had learned, deeper than the habits that had shaped him, deeper than his love for the master, deeper than his very will to survive; and when, in the moment of his uncertainty, Collie nipped him and ran off, he turned and followed her. The master rode alone that day; and in the woods, side by side, White Fang ran with Collie, just as his mother, Kiche, and old One Eye had run many years before in the quiet northern forest.

Chapter V: The Sleeping Wolf

Around this time, newspapers were filled with stories about the bold escape of a prisoner from San Quentin prison. He was a violent man. He had been poorly formed from the beginning. He hadn't been born properly, and the shaping he received from society hadn't helped him at all. Society's influence is cruel, and this man was a perfect example of what it could create. He was an animal—a human animal, certainly, but such a frightening creature that he could best be described as a predator.

In San Quentin prison, he had shown himself to be beyond reform. No amount of punishment could crush his defiant spirit.

He would rather die in silent rage, fighting until his final breath, than live in defeat. The harder he resisted, the more brutally society treated him, and this cruelty only served to fuel his fierce nature. Straitjackets, starvation, beatings, and violent attacks were completely wrong for someone like Jim Hall, yet this was exactly what he endured. This harsh treatment had been his reality since he was a vulnerable young boy in the slums of San Francisco— malleable like soft clay in society's hands, ready to be shaped into something meaningful.

It was during Jim Hall's third prison sentence that he met a guard who was nearly as brutal as he was. The guard treated him unjustly, told lies about him to the warden, took away his earned privileges, and tormented him constantly. The only difference between the two men was that the guard had a set of keys and a gun. Jim Hall possessed nothing but his bare hands and his teeth. However, one day he attacked the guard and bit into his throat like a wild animal from the jungle.

After this, Jim Hall was sent to live in the solitary confinement cell. He remained there for three years. The cell was made entirely of iron—the floor, the walls, and the ceiling. He never left this cell. He never saw the sky or felt sunshine. Daytime became a dim twilight, and night turned into complete, silent darkness. He existed in an iron tomb, buried alive. He saw no human faces and spoke to no one. When his food was pushed through to him, he snarled like a wild beast. He despised everything. For days and nights, he roared his fury at the world. For weeks and months, he made no sound at all, sitting in the black silence as it consumed his very soul. He had become both man and monster, as terrifying a creature of fear as any that ever appeared in the nightmares of a deranged mind.

And then, one night, he broke free. The guards insisted it couldn't be done, but the cell stood empty nonetheless, with a dead guard's body lying half inside and half outside. Two more dead guards traced his path through the prison to the outer walls, and he had killed them with his bare hands to keep silent.

He carried the weapons taken from the dead guards—a walking armory that raced through the mountains while society's organized forces chased him. A substantial bounty had been placed on his head. Greedy landowners pursued him with shotguns. His death could eliminate a mortgage or fund a child's education. Civic-minded residents grabbed their rifles and joined the hunt. A pack of bloodhounds tracked the trail of his wounded feet. And the detective forces of the law, society's paid enforcers, using telephone, telegraph, and special trains, stayed on his path day and night.

Sometimes they encountered him, and men confronted him with heroic courage, or they panicked and rushed through barbed-wire fences, much to the entertainment of the general public reading these reports over their morning breakfast. Following such confrontations, the dead and injured were transported back to the towns, and their positions were taken by men enthusiastic about joining the manhunt.

Jim Hall vanished without a trace. The bloodhounds searched desperately but couldn't pick up his trail. Innocent ranchers living in isolated valleys found themselves confronted by armed men who forced them to prove their identities, while bounty hunters eager for reward money claimed to have found Jim Hall's body on numerous mountainsides.

In the meantime, the newspapers were read at Sierra Vista, not so much with interest as with anxiety. The women were afraid. Judge Scott dismissed the concerns and laughed, but not with good reason, for it was during his final days on the bench that Jim Hall had stood before him and received his sentence. And in the open courtroom, before all present, Jim Hall had declared that the day would come when he would take revenge on the Judge who had sentenced him.

For once, Jim Hall was right. He was innocent of the crime he had been sentenced for. In the language of criminals and law enforcement, this was a case of "railroading." Jim Hall was being "railroaded" to prison for a crime he didn't commit. Due to his two previous convictions, Judge Scott sentenced him to fifty years.

Judge Scott didn't know everything, and he had no idea that he was part of a police conspiracy, that the evidence had been fabricated and witnesses had lied under oath, that Jim Hall was innocent of the crime he was accused of. Meanwhile, Jim Hall didn't realize that Judge Scott was simply unaware of the truth. Jim Hall was convinced that the judge knew exactly what was happening and was working together with the police to carry out this terrible injustice. So when Judge Scott pronounced the sentence of fifty years of living death, Jim Hall, filled with hatred for the entire society that had wronged him, jumped up and flew into a rage in the courtroom until half a dozen of his blue-uniformed enemies dragged him down. To him, Judge Scott represented the cornerstone of this system of injustice, and he poured out all his fury on Judge Scott and shouted threats of the revenge he would one day take. Then Jim Hall went to his living death . . . and escaped.

White Fang was completely unaware of all this. However, he and Alice, his master's wife, shared a secret between them. Every night, once everyone at Sierra Vista had gone to sleep, she would get up and quietly let White Fang inside to sleep in the large hall. White Fang wasn't a house dog, and he wasn't allowed to sleep indoors, so each morning she would sneak downstairs early and let him back outside before the rest of the family woke up.

On one such night, while everyone in the house was sleeping, White Fang woke up and remained completely still. He quietly sniffed the air and understood the scent it carried of an unfamiliar person nearby. His ears picked up the sounds of this stranger moving around. White Fang didn't burst into angry barking. That wasn't his nature. The intruder moved quietly, but White Fang moved even more silently, since he wore no clothing that might brush against his body and make noise. He followed without making a sound. In the wilderness, he had stalked prey that was extremely cautious and alert, so he understood the value of catching someone off guard.

The unfamiliar god stopped at the bottom of the grand staircase and listened carefully, while White Fang remained completely motionless, as still as death itself, as he observed and waited. That staircase led upward to his beloved master and to his master's most treasured belongings. White Fang's hair stood on end, but he continued to wait. The stranger's foot rose. He was starting to climb.

At that moment, White Fang attacked. He gave no warning and didn't snarl before making his move. He launched his body into the air in a leap that brought him down on the stranger's back. White Fang gripped the man's shoulders with his front paws while simultaneously sinking his teeth into the back of the man's neck. He held on for a brief moment, just long enough to pull the man over backward. They both crashed to the ground together. White Fang jumped away, and as the man tried to get back up, White Fang was on him again with his cutting fangs.

Sierra Vista woke up in panic. The sounds coming from downstairs were like twenty demons fighting each other. Gunshots rang out. A man's voice screamed once in terror and pain. There was fierce snarling and growling, and above it all came the sound of furniture and glass being smashed and destroyed.

But almost as quickly as it had started, the disturbance faded away. The fight had lasted no more than three minutes. The terrified household gathered at the top of the stairs. From below, as if from a pit of darkness, rose a gurgling noise, like air bubbling through water. At times this gurgling became hissing, almost like a whistle. But this sound, too, quickly faded and stopped. Then nothing emerged from the darkness except the heavy breathing of some creature desperately gasping for air.

Weedon Scott pressed a button, and light flooded the staircase and downstairs hallway. He and Judge Scott then carefully made their way down, revolvers in their hands. Their caution proved unnecessary. White Fang had completed his task. Among the wreckage of overturned and broken furniture, a man lay partially on his side with his face concealed by his arm. Weedon Scott leaned down, moved the arm aside, and turned the man's face upward. A torn throat revealed how he had died.

"Jim Hall," Judge Scott said, and father and son exchanged meaningful glances.

Then they turned their attention to White Fang. He was also lying on his side. His eyes were closed, but his eyelids lifted slightly as he tried to look at them while they leaned over him, and his tail moved noticeably in a weak attempt to wag. Weedon Scott gently patted him, and a low growl rumbled from his throat in acknowledgment. However, it was a faint growl at best, and it soon faded away. His eyelids grew heavy and closed completely, and his entire body appeared to relax and settle flat against the floor.

"He's completely exhausted, poor devil," muttered the master.

"We'll see about that," declared the Judge, as he headed toward the telephone.

"To be honest, he has about a one in a thousand chance of surviving," the surgeon declared after working on White Fang for an hour and a half.

Dawn was breaking through the windows and dimming the electric lights. With the exception of the children, the whole family had gathered around the surgeon to hear his verdict.

"One broken hind leg," he continued. "Three broken ribs, with at least one having punctured the lungs. He's lost almost all the blood in his body. There's a strong possibility of internal injuries. Something must have trampled him. Not to mention three bullet wounds that went straight through him. One chance in a thousand is actually being optimistic. He doesn't have a chance in ten thousand."

"But he can't miss any opportunity that could help him," Judge Scott declared. "Don't worry about the cost. Get him an X-ray—whatever it takes. Weedon, send a telegram to San Francisco right away for Doctor Nichols. I'm not criticizing you, doctor, you understand; but he needs every possible advantage."

The surgeon smiled with understanding. "Of course I get it. He deserves everything we can possibly do for him. You need to care for him the same way you'd care for a human being, like a sick child. And remember what I said about keeping track of his temperature. I'll return at ten o'clock."

White Fang received the care he needed. Judge Scott's suggestion to hire a professional nurse was angrily rejected by the girls, who took on the responsibility themselves. And White Fang survived against the one-in-ten-thousand odds that the surgeon had given him.

The doctor couldn't be blamed for his poor judgment. Throughout his entire career, he had treated and performed surgery on the pampered people of civilization, who lived protected lives and came from many generations of protected ancestors. When compared to White Fang, these people were weak and soft, holding onto life with a feeble grasp. White Fang had emerged directly from the wilderness, where the frail die young and no one receives protection. Neither his father nor his mother possessed any frailty, nor did the generations that came before them. An iron-strong body and the fierce energy of the wilderness were what White Fang had inherited, and he held onto life—all of him and every piece of him, in both soul and body—with the same fierce determination that had once belonged to all wild creatures.

Trapped like a prisoner, unable to move because of the plaster casts and bandages that held him, White Fang endured the passing weeks. He slept for long stretches and dreamed extensively, while an endless parade of memories from the Northland flowed through his mind. All the spirits of his past returned to be with him. He lived once more in the den with Kiche, crawled fearfully to Grey Beaver's knees to offer his loyalty, and fled for his life from Lip-lip and the entire howling chaos of the puppy pack.

He ran once more through the quiet, chasing his prey during the hungry months; and once more he led the pack, with Mit-sah and Grey Beaver's whips cracking behind him, their voices shouting "Ra! Raa!" whenever they reached a tight spot and the team bunched together like a fan to pass through. He relived all his time with Beauty Smith and the battles he had endured. During these moments he whined and growled in his sleep, and those who watched him said his dreams were troubled.

But there was one specific nightmare that tormented him— the rattling, clanging monsters of electric cars that appeared to him as enormous screaming lynxes. He would hide behind a screen of bushes, waiting for a squirrel to wander far enough from its tree sanctuary onto the ground. Then, when he leaped out to attack it, the squirrel would transform into an electric car, threatening and terrifying, looming over him like a mountain, shrieking and clanging and shooting sparks at him. The same thing happened when he confronted the hawk swooping down from the sky. Down from the blue it would dive, and as it descended upon him, it would change into the ever-present electric car. Or sometimes, he would find himself in Beauty Smith's pen. Outside the enclosure, men would be gathering, and he understood that a fight was about to begin. He watched the door for his opponent to enter. The door would swing open, and the dreadful electric car would be shoved in toward him. This happened a thousand times, and each time the fear it caused was as intense and overwhelming as ever.

Then came the day when the final bandage and the last plaster cast were removed. It was a celebration. Everyone from Sierra Vista had gathered around. The master scratched his ears, and he made his affectionate growling sound. The master's wife called him the "Blessed Wolf," a name that was enthusiastically adopted and all the women began calling him the Blessed Wolf.

He attempted to stand up, and after multiple tries, he collapsed from weakness. He had been lying down for so long that his muscles had lost their coordination, and all their strength had drained away. He felt somewhat ashamed of his weakness, as if he were somehow letting down the gods in the duty he owed them. Because of this feeling, he made tremendous efforts to get up, and finally he managed to stand on his four legs, wobbling and rocking back and forth.

"The Blessed Wolf!" the women called out together.

Judge Scott looked at them with a triumphant expression.

"You've said it yourselves," he declared. "That's exactly what I've been arguing all along. No ordinary dog could have accomplished what he did. He's a wolf."

"A Blessed Wolf," the Judge's wife corrected.

"Yes, Blessed Wolf," the Judge agreed. "And from now on, that's what I'll call him."

"He'll need to learn how to walk again," the surgeon explained. "He might as well begin right now. It won't cause him any harm. Take him outside."

And outside he went, like a king, with all of Sierra Vista surrounding him and caring for him. He was extremely weak, and when he made it to the lawn he lay down and rested for a moment.

Then the procession began moving forward, with small bursts of energy flowing into White Fang's muscles as he exercised them and blood started circulating through them again. They reached the stables, and there in the entrance lay Collie, with half a dozen chubby puppies playing around her in the sunlight.

White Fang watched with curious eyes. Collie growled a warning at him, and he made sure to stay far away. The master used his foot to gently push one tumbling puppy closer to him. White Fang's fur stood on end with suspicion, but the master reassured him that everything was fine. Collie, held securely in one of the women's arms, watched him with jealous eyes and growled a warning that everything was definitely not fine.

The puppy lay stretched out in front of him. He tilted his ears forward and observed it with curiosity. Then their noses met, and he felt the puppy's warm little tongue on his cheek. White Fang's tongue emerged without him understanding why, and he licked the puppy's face.

The gods responded with enthusiastic applause and delighted shouts at his performance. This caught him off guard, and he gazed at them with a confused expression. Soon his fatigue took over, and he settled down on the ground, ears perked up and head tilted to one side as he observed the puppy. The rest of the puppies began tumbling toward him, much to Collie's annoyance, and he solemnly allowed them to climb and roll all over him. Initially, while the gods continued their praise, he showed hints of his former shyness and clumsiness. These feelings faded as the puppies kept playing and roughhousing around him, and he rested there with eyes half-closed and patient, dozing peacefully in the warm sunlight.

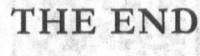

THE END

Thank You For Reading

You've Just Read a Piece of the Greatest Library Ever Rebuilt

Thank you for reading.

This book is one of thousands we're restoring, reimagining, and translating as part of the **Modern Library of Alexandria** — a global movement to preserve and share humanity's most important ideas.

What was once lost to fire and time is now rising again — not just as memory, but as living, breathing knowledge, freely accessible to all.

What You Can Do Next:

- **Keep Reading.**

  Discover more legendary works — in beautiful print, audiobook, or digital form — at LibraryofAlexandria.com.

- **Build Your Own Library.**

  Every title is available as a paperback, hardcover, or collectible boxset — at true printing cost. Craft a personal library worthy of display.

- **Spread the Light.**

  Share this book. Tell others about the movement. Help us translate every timeless work into every language, so no reader is ever left behind.

By finishing this book, you've already taken part in something extraordinary.

Join us at LibraryofAlexandria.com

Together, we're rebuilding the greatest library the world has ever known.

With appreciation,

The Modern Library of Alexandria Team

Visit:
www.libraryofalexandria.com
Or scan the code below:

www.ingramcontent.com/pod-product-compliance
Lightning Source LLC
Chambersburg PA
CBHW011405010726

47495CB00009B/2789